Dish of the Day

Jane Humphreys

By the same author:

Dish of the Day: 80 Popular Recipes

DISH OF THE DAY
MORE POPULAR RECIPES

JANE HUMPHREYS

Line drawings and cover illustration by Anny King

Caterpillar Books
1992

First published in 1992

© 1992 Jane Humphreys

All rights reserved. No part of this publication may be published, reproduced, stored in a retrieval system, or transmitted, in any form or by any means, electronic, mechanical, photocopying, recording or otherwise, without the prior permission of the copyright owner.

*To my mother and father
chief cook and head gardener*

ISBN 0 9519604 0 7

Published by Caterpillar Books, Lower Failand, Near Bristol, Avon BS8 3SS.

Typeset, printed and bound by J W Arrowsmith Ltd, Winterstoke Road, Bristol BS3 2NT.

CONTENTS

Preface	6
Starters	7
Soups	27
Fish	45
Poultry and game	65
Meat	83
Pasta, rice and beans	105
Vegetables	121
Salads	139
Puddings	153
Cakes and biscuits	171
Preserves	189
Index	205

PREFACE

During the past few years I have published over 1,000 recipes in the Bristol Evening Post and this collection represents some of my own favourites and others that have been popular with readers.

My attitude to cooking is that we should not be intimidated by what the media food gurus tell us, but that we should cook what we like to eat. If we are governed by our own tastes, the time available to us, and the money in our purses, we can very quickly develop a delicious repertoire of dishes that are quick and easy to prepare and which do not cost the earth.

All the recipes in the book have been made in my own kitchen and tested by my merry band of tasters: Robert, Henry, William, George and Edward, whom I should like to thank, especially for the occasions when dishes have not gone quite right. And I am grateful to all those friends and relations who have also acted as guinea pigs. Thanks are also due to the many Evening Post readers who write in with their helpful comments.

I am indebted to British Meat for ideas for some of the recipes in the meat chapter.

Measurements

Measurements are given in imperial and metric; both work well but should not be mixed in the same recipe.

Vegetables, unless stated otherwise, should be of a medium size. Spoon measurements should be level, unless stated otherwise.

All recipes serve 4 people unless stated otherwise.

Jane Humphreys

STARTERS

Artichokes · Asparagus · Stilton · Mussels · Sardines

STARTERS

If you are preparing a special meal, the first course is in a way the most important. It doesn't need to be too substantial, because you want your guests to enjoy the main course, but it should look attractive and make people want to sit down and eat.

A pretty presentation and neat finishing touches are more important at this stage of the meal than later on, when people will be relaxed and chattering to each other, and will possibly be less observant of what is in front of them.

This doesn't mean you have to create complicated dishes. Simple starters are best, served in small portions that leave people wanting more! Things that can be made the night before, placed on plates, and refrigerated until needed are jolly useful, but remember to take them out the fridge in time, or the food will be too cold to have any flavour.

It's best to make a starter that contrasts with the main course; don't serve pâté if you're offering red meat, don't start with seafood and then follow it with fish. And think of colour; don't present a pale mousse followed by chicken followed by lemon ice cream or your guests will die of boredom.

Many of the recipes in this section may also be used for snacks or lunches, serving fewer people.

Anchoïade (Mediterranean anchovy dip)
Artichokes vinaigrette
Asparagus with lemon and herb butter
Avocados with crab
Cacik (Turkish yogurt soup)
Cheese puffs
Cheesy tricorns
Cheesy shrimps
Chicken liver and walnut pâté
Chicken livers in sour cream
Coriander mushrooms
Cucumber and crab salad
Dips for parties:
  Avocado and onion
  Garlic and herb
  Hummus
  Tuna and chick pea pâté
Herb and Stilton pâté
Lemon and sardine pâté
Moules marinière (mussels in white wine)
Mussels in tomato sauce
Pâté en croûte (home made pâté in a puff pastry crust)
Rough country pâté
Salade Niçoise
Smoked mackerel and dill pâté
Spring rolls
Stuffed mushrooms
Stuffed plaice fillets
Vegetable crudités
Whisky prawns

ANCHOÏADE
Mediterranean anchovy dip

2 × 2 oz tins anchovies in brine (110 g)
2 cloves garlic, crushed
2 tablespoons fresh parsley, chopped
2 tablespoons brandy
2 tablespoons olive oil
freshly ground black pepper

Rinse the anchovies in cold water to get rid of some of the salt, and then pat them dry on kitchen paper. Place them in the bowl of your food processor or the goblet of a liquidiser, add the garlic and parsley, and whizz up until smooth. Add the brandy and olive oil, and process again. Season with freshly ground black pepper. Serve spread on thin slices of French bread, toasted on one side only, or serve as a dip with thinly sliced raw vegetables. Anchoïade keeps well in the fridge for several days, although the flavour becomes less intense.
Serves 4–6.

ARTICHOKES VINAIGRETTE

4 globe artichokes
6 tablespoons olive oil
2 tablespoons white wine vinegar
1 teaspoon salt
1 teaspoon English mustard powder
freshly ground black pepper

Using a pair of scissors, snip off the pointed tops of the leaves. Dig out and discard the hairy "choke" by cutting around the base of the stalk with a sharp knife, then ease it out. Place in a large pan half filled with boiling lightly salted water and boil for 35–40 minutes or until the artichokes feel soft. Drain well. Make the dressing by whisking the remaining ingredients together, or by shaking them well in a screw topped jar. Serve the artichokes warm or cold, with a small bowl of vinaigrette by each plate. Give everyone a finger bowl, a napkin, and an extra plate for discarded leaves.

ASPARAGUS WITH LEMON AND HERB BUTTER

Asparagus is one of the delights of early summer. Serve it on its own, with a simple sauce like this one, and give your fellow diners fingerbowls or napkins as eating it tends to be a messy business.

> 1 bundle fresh asparagus
> 4 oz unsalted butter (110 g)
> grated zest of two lemons
> $\frac{1}{2}$ teaspoon salt
> freshly ground black pepper
> 1 tablespoon French tarragon leaves, finely chopped

Cut the woody ends off the asparagus and reserve for soup. Steam or boil the tips for a few minutes until just tender. Meanwhile, melt the butter and stir in the lemon zest, salt, pepper to taste, and tarragon leaves. Serve the asparagus hot, with the buttery sauce poured over and accompanied by thin slices of brown bread to mop up the juices.

AVOCADOS WITH CRAB

> 8 oz white crab meat, fresh, frozen, or tinned (225 g)
> 2 tablespoons bought mayonnaise
> 1 tablespoon lemon juice
> 2 tablespoons single cream
> $\frac{1}{4}$ teaspoon cayenne pepper
> $\frac{1}{2}$ teaspoon salt
> freshly ground black pepper
> 2 ripe avocados
>
> to serve:
> 1 lemon, quartered
> shredded lettuce leaves
> thin toast

Put the crab meat, mayonnaise, lemon juice, cream and seasoning into a large bowl and mix thoroughly. Chill until ready to serve. To serve, halve the avocados, remove the stones (jabbing a sharp knife into them and twisting out is the easiest way), and pile the crab mixture into the four hollows. Serve each avocado on a bed of shredded lettuce with a lemon quarter and thin slices of toast. Do not cut the avocados too soon or they will discolour.

CACIK
Turkish yogurt soup

1 pint thick Greek natural yogurt (600 ml)
2 fat cloves garlic, crushed
1 tablespoon fresh dill or mint, chopped
salt and freshly ground black pepper
1 large cucumber, roughly grated or finely chopped

Beat the yogurt, garlic, dill or mint, and seasoning together and leave in the fridge for a couple of hours for the flavours to develop. Put the chopped or grated cucumber in a sieve over a bowl, to allow the excess water to drip out. Tip the cucumber on to kitchen paper, pat dry, then stir it into the yogurt just before serving. Serve as a chilled soup or as an accompaniment to a spicy meal.

CHEESE PUFFS

2 oz unsalted butter (55 g)
$\frac{1}{4}$ pint water (150 ml)
$2\frac{1}{2}$ oz plain flour, sifted (60 g)
2 fresh eggs
2 oz farmhouse Cheddar, grated (55 g)
oil for frying

Put the water and butter into a small non-stick saucepan, melt the butter and bring to the boil. Tip all the flour in at once and mix well. Beat with a wooden spoon until smooth, then take off the heat. Leave to cool, then beat in the eggs one at a time until the mixture is glossy. Stir in the cheese and seasoning to make a stiff and sticky mixture. Now heat the oil in a saucepan or deep fryer and take heaped teaspoonfuls of the mixture and drop them into the oil. Fry until brown and crunchy on all sides. The puffs will swell up and be crunchy on the outside and soft and cheesy inside. Fry in batches if necessary, keeping the first ones warm on crumpled kitchen paper in the oven.
Makes 16.

Variations
Try flavouring with herbs, grated onion, or pop a prawn or shrimp into each ball before frying.

CHEESY SHRIMPS

4 oz shrimps (or prawns) (110 g)
4 oz farmhouse Cheddar, grated (110 g)
3 eggs, hard boiled, shelled and chopped small
1 oz plain flour, sifted (25 g)
1½ oz butter (40 g)
½ pint milk (300 ml)
salt and freshly ground black pepper

Start by making the sauce: over a medium heat, gently melt the butter, stir in the flour, cook gently for one minute, then incorporate the milk little by little until the sauce is smooth and glossy. Add seasoning, then cook the sauce gently for a couple of minutes more. Remove the pan from the heat, add the shrimps, chopped eggs and three-quarters of the cheese. Allow the cheese to melt, then put back on the hob and allow to simmer gently for about five minutes. Pour into four individual heatproof dishes, sprinkle the rest of the cheese on top, and grill until golden. Serve with thin slices of wholemeal bread.

CHEESY TRICORNS

4 oz wholemeal flour (110 g)
4 oz plain flour (110 g)
4 oz margarine (110 g)
1 oz farmhouse Cheddar, grated (25 g)
½ teaspoon English mustard powder
1 egg, beaten
2 teaspoons ready made Dijon mustard
2 tablespoons fresh parsley, chopped
2 oz Edam cheese cut into tiny triangles (55 g)
2 tablespoons sesame seeds
milk for brushing

Make the pastry by rubbing in the fat and flours, add the Cheddar and English mustard powder, and then stir in the egg and enough cold water to form a stiff dough. Chill, then roll out and cut into 50 2 inch (5 mm) rounds. Mix the Dijon mustard and parsley together and spread a little in the centre of each circle. Place a triangle of Edam in the middle. Brush the edges of each circle with water, bring the sides up to make a three cornered shape, and press together over the cheese. Brush with milk and sprinkle with the seeds. Bake at Gas 6, 400 deg F, 200 deg C for 15–20 minutes. Serve hot.

CHICKEN LIVER, MUSHROOM AND AND WALNUT PATE

1 oz butter (25 g)
1 small onion, peeled and finely chopped
8 oz chicken livers, rinsed and chopped (225 g)
1 clove garlic, crushed
1 bay leaf, crushed
2 oz walnuts, finely chopped (55 g)
4 oz mushrooms (110 g)
1 tablespoon red wine
salt and freshly ground black pepper

Melt half the butter in a frying pan, soften the onion, then add the chicken livers, garlic and bay leaf. Fry gently, stirring now and then, for about ten minutes. Remove the chicken livers from the frying pan, discard the bay leaf, and place them in the goblet of a liquidiser with the finely chopped walnuts. Melt the remaining butter and sweat the mushrooms, then add them to the ingredients in the liquidiser, add wine and seasoning, and process until you reach the desired consistency. Spoon into a small shallow bowl, or four ramekins, decorate with bay leaves or four halved walnuts, and allow to get quite cold in the fridge. Serve with toast.

CHICKEN LIVERS IN SOUR CREAM

2 tablespoons corn oil
1 small onion, peeled and finely chopped
1 clove garlic, crushed
8 oz chicken livers (225 g)
4 oz mushrooms, wiped and sliced (110 g)
$\frac{1}{4}$ pint sour cream (150 ml)
1 tablespoon plain flour
salt and freshly ground black pepper

to garnish:
fresh parsley, chopped

Heat the oil in a heavy-bottomed frying pan, then add the onion and garlic and soften gently. Meanwhile, chop the chicken livers roughly. Add them to the pan and turn up the heat a little. When they are browned on all sides, add the mushrooms, and cook for a few more minutes, stirring well. Now stir in the flour and cook for one minute. Add the sour cream and allow to heat through gently. Do not boil. Season, and serve hot, garnished with chopped parsley and with thin slices of toast.

CORIANDER MUSHROOMS

2 tablespoons olive oil
1 medium onion, peeled and chopped
1 clove garlic, crushed
2 tablespoons tomato purée
½ pint red wine (300 ml)
a few parsley stalks and a sprig of fresh thyme
1 tablespoon coriander seeds, crushed
1 teaspoon sugar
grated zest of an orange
1 lb button mushrooms, wiped (450 g)
4 fresh tomatoes, skinned and quartered
salt and freshly ground black pepper

to garnish:
fresh coriander leaves, chopped

Heat the oil in a large frying pan, then add the onion and garlic, and soften. Stir in the tomato purée, wine, herbs, coriander seeds, sugar, orange zest, and seasoning. Bring to the boil, then turn down the heat, and add the mushrooms and chopped tomatoes, and cook gently for 10–15 minutes until the mushrooms are just tender. Remove the herbs and spoon the mushrooms and juices into a serving bowl. Chill in the fridge. Garnish with chopped coriander leaves before serving.

CUCUMBER AND CRAB SALAD

8 oz fresh white crab meat (225 g)
2 tablespoons bought mayonnaise
1 tablespoon lemon juice
½ a cucumber
6 tablespoons olive oil
1 tablespoon white wine vinegar or lemon juice
salt and freshly ground black pepper

to garnish:
paprika and fresh dill

Combine crab meat, mayonnaise, salt and pepper, and add lemon juice to taste. (If you cannot obtain fresh crab, frozen or tinned is acceptable, but must be allowed to drain first.) Chill for an hour or so. Make the vinaigrette dressing by whisking the olive oil and vinegar together with salt and pepper to taste. When ready to serve, slice the cucumber as thinly as possible and arrange around the edges of a serving plate or four small plates, and sprinkle with the vinaigrette. Pile the crab meat into the centre, sprinkle with paprika and garnish with fresh dill.

DIPS FOR SPECIAL OCCASIONS

If you have a food processor, these dips are simplicity itself to make. You can serve them with thin strips of fresh vegetables and crisps or savoury biscuits at parties or pre-dinner drinks, and you can also offer them as a starter at an informal meal.

AVOCADO AND ONION

2 ripe avocados
$\frac{1}{2}$ a small onion, finely grated
juice of a lemon
2 teaspoons grated lemon zest
3 oz cream cheese (75 g)
salt, pepper, cayenne pepper

to garnish:
paprika

Halve the avocados, remove the stones, and scoop out the flesh. Mash the flesh with all the other ingredients, adding salt, pepper and cayenne to taste. Sprinkle with a little paprika before serving. This dip discolours if you make it too far ahead, but since you can whizz it up in seconds in the food processor, you shouldn't really need to prepare it hours in advance.
Serves 4–6.

GARLIC AND HERB

4 oz skimmed milk soft cheese (110 g)
4 oz full fat soft cheese (110 g)
2 tablespoons plain yogurt
3 fat cloves garlic, peeled and crushed
salt and freshly ground black pepper
1 heaped tablespoon fresh herbs, finely chopped

to garnish:
sprigs of fresh herbs

Crush the garlic cloves, then beat or mash all the ingredients together until well combined. Chill, covered, in the fridge until needed, and then garnish with sprigs of fresh herbs.

HUMMUS

8 oz dried chick peas (225 g)
4 tablespoons tahini paste
$\frac{1}{4}$ pint olive oil (150 ml)
2 cloves garlic, crushed
juice of a lemon
salt and freshly ground black pepper

to garnish:
black olives and fresh mint leaves

Cover the chick peas in boiling water, then simmer for an hour or so until tender. Drain, reserving the cooking liquid. Place all the ingredients in a blender, reserving one tablespoon of the olive oil, and process until smooth. Add a little of the cooking liquid if the hummus is too stiff, but do not make it runny. Spoon into a serving dish, sprinkle the reserved olive oil over the top, and garnish with black olives and fresh mint leaves. Serve with warmed pitta bread. (Note: to save time, you can use two 14 oz (400 g) tins of chick peas, drained.)
Serves 6–8.

TUNA AND CHICK PEA PATE

4 oz dried chick peas (110 g)
1 small onion, peeled and chopped
1 clove garlic, crushed
7 oz tin tuna fish in brine, drained (200 g)
2 oz butter (55 g)
juice of $\frac{1}{2}$ a lemon
1–3 tablespoons bought mayonnaise
1–3 tablespoons double cream
2 tablespoons fresh parsley, chopped
salt and freshly ground black pepper

to garnish:
fresh parsley

Place the chick peas in a saucepan, cover with boiling water, and simmer until tender; this may take an hour or more. Drain them and blend with the onion, garlic, tuna, butter, lemon juice and a tablespoon each of cream and mayonnaise. Keep adding cream and mayonnaise until you reach the desired consistency. Season with salt and freshly ground black pepper, and chill before serving. Serve garnished with parsley and offered with French bread or pitta bread. (Note: a 14 oz (400 g) tin of chick peas, drained, may be used if time is short.)
Serves 8.

HERB AND STILTON PATE

Stilton works well in this pâté but you can use Danish Blue or other soft blue cheeses, or a combination of odds and ends from the fridge.

    5 oz Stilton (150 g)
    5 oz farmhouse Cheddar (150 g)
    5 tablespoons double cream
    2 tablespoons fresh thyme leaves, basil, parsley and sage, mixed
      equally and chopped finely
    1 teaspoon garlic salt

    to garnish:
    paprika and small sprigs of thyme

Grate the Cheddar cheese very finely and mash the Stilton. Mix the two cheeses together, then beat in the cream, herbs and garlic salt. Spoon into a pretty glass bowl and chill in the fridge. Serve with thin, hot toast and crunchy celery sticks.

ITALIAN TUNA SALAD

    8 oz dried haricot or flageolet beans (225 g)
    1 bay leaf, crushed
    1 sprig thyme
    2 cloves garlic
    7 oz tin tuna fish in brine (200 g)
    1 onion, peeled and finely chopped
    12 stoned black olives
    salt and freshly ground black pepper

    for the dressing:
    juice of $\frac{1}{2}$ a lemon
    4 tablespoons olive oil
    1 teaspoon English mustard powder
    1 clove garlic, crushed

Soak the beans overnight in plenty of cold water. Then bring them to the boil in fresh water and simmer, together with the bay leaf, thyme, and garlic for at least half an hour until they are tender. Drain, discarding cooking liquor and herbs. Place the beans in a large bowl. Make the dressing by whisking the ingredients together until well combined. Pour over the warm beans and toss well. Drain and flake the tuna, stir this in with most of the olives, and add salt and pepper to taste. Sprinkle the parsley over the top and garnish with the remaining olives.
Serves 6.

LEMON AND SARDINE PATE

2 cans sardines in oil
4 oz butter (110 g)
4 oz low fat cream cheese (110 g)
juice of ½ a large lemon
1 teaspoon Dijon mustard
salt and freshly ground black pepper

to garnish:
sprigs of parsley

Beat the sardines with their oil, butter and cream cheese until well blended (a food processor or liquidiser will do this in seconds). Divide between ramekins or lemon shells. To serve, decorate with sprigs of parsley and offer with thinly sliced hot toast. Serves 6–8.

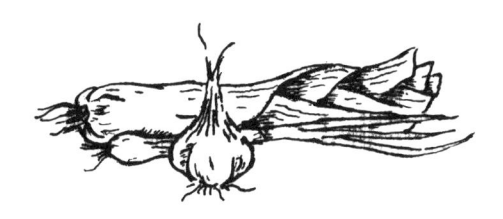

MOULES MARINIERE
Mussels in white wine

4 pints fresh mussels (2.3 litres)
1 onion, peeled and finely chopped
2 cloves garlic, crushed
2 sprigs each fresh thyme and parsley
½ pint dry white wine (300 ml)
freshly ground black pepper

Place all the ingredients, except the mussels and a sprig each of the herbs, in a large pan and boil hard, uncovered, until the wine has nearly reduced by half. Meanwhile, rinse the mussels under running water and trim off all bits and pieces. Discard any open mussels, then tip into the pan. Cover with a lid, and cook until the mussels open—no more than five minutes. Remove the mussels, discard any that have not opened, and keep warm on a serving dish. Strain the cooking liquor, return to the pan and boil until reduced by half again, then pour over the mussels, garnish with the reserved thyme and parsley, and serve at once, with plenty of crusty bread to mop up the juices.

MUSSELS IN TOMATO SAUCE

8 oz shelled mussels (225 g)
2 tablespoons olive oil
1 clove garlic, crushed
1 medium onion, peeled and finely chopped
14 oz tin Italian tomatoes (400 g)
salt and freshly ground black pepper
1 tablespoon fresh parsley, tarragon or basil, chopped

Heat the oil, soften the onion and garlic, then add the tomatoes, a little salt, and lots of pepper. Simmer gently until you have a nice thick sauce; this will take about half an hour. Add the mussels and herbs five minutes before you are ready to eat, and allow the mussels to heat through. Do not overcook or they will be rubbery. Serve in ramekins or small bowls with plenty of crusty bread to mop up the sauce. Serves 2–3.

PATE EN CROUTE
Home made pâté in a puff pastry crust

1 oz butter (25 g)
1 small onion, peeled and finely chopped
1 clove garlic, crushed
8 oz chicken livers (225 g)
8 oz mushrooms, wiped (225 g)
1 sprig thyme
1 bay leaf, crushed
freshly ground black pepper
8 oz puff pastry, defrosted (225 g)

to glaze:
milk or beaten egg

Rinse the chicken livers, pat dry, and roughly chop them. Melt half the butter in a frying pan and gently soften the onion and garlic. Add the chicken livers and brown. Roughly chop the mushrooms and add to the pan with the rest of the butter, thyme, bay leaf, and black pepper. Cook gently, stirring now and then, for ten minutes. Remove the herbs. Transfer to a food processor or blender and process to a fairly rough consistency. Allow to cool a little, then roll out the pastry to form a rectangle about 8 × 10 inches (20 × 25 cm), and spread the pâté down the middle, leaving a border at each end. Roll up, brushing the edges with water and pressing firmly together. Brush with beaten egg or milk, and bake at Gas 6, 400 deg F, 200 deg C for 25–30 minutes, or until the pastry is risen and golden (turn down the heat after the first ten minutes if necessary.) Serve hot or cold.
Serves 6–8.

PRAWN COCKTAIL WITH BLUE CHEESE DRESSING

This is a variation on the popular but predictable prawn cocktail, and it's just as easy to make.

8 oz cooked and peeled prawns (225 g)
4 prawns in shell
4 tablespoons good bought mayonnaise
4 oz Danish Blue cheese (110 g)
juice of $\frac{1}{2}$ a lemon
1 crisp lettuce heart
paprika
4 lemon slices

If the prawns are frozen, make sure they are properly defrosted. Let them drain on kitchen paper and pat them dry. Wash the lettuce, pat it dry, then shred finely and divide between four wide mouthed wine glasses. Beat the cheese until soft, then beat in the mayonnaise and lemon juice. Mix the prawns in gently. Divide between the glasses. Sprinkle with paprika. Cut a slit in each lemon slice and suspend on the rim of the glass. Suspend a whole prawn in its shell on the rim of the glass. Serve at once. For a change, add cucumber or finely chopped celery to the lettuce base, and a sliced scallop or two makes the cocktail rather special.

ROUGH COUNTRY PATE

12 oz lamb's liver (350 g)
12 oz lean belly pork (350 g)
1 small onion, peeled and finely chopped
1 clove garlic, crushed
1 egg, beaten
1 tablespoon fresh parsley, finely chopped
salt and freshly ground black pepper
8–10 rashers streaky bacon

Mince the liver and belly pork to a fairly coarse consistency. Combine all the ingredients except the streaky bacon. Line a 2 lb (1 kg) loaf tin with stretched out rashers of bacon, pack in the pâté mixture, and fold any spare strips of bacon over the top. Cover with foil, then place in a roasting tin half filled with hot water, and cook at Gas 4, 350 deg F, 180 deg C for 45–60 minutes. The pâté should shrink away from the sides of the tin when it is cooked. Leave to get cold in the tin, then turn out and serve cut into slices.
Serves 6–8.

SALADE NICOISE

2 fresh eggs
4 oz French beans (110 g)
8 crisp lettuce leaves
½ a cucumber
6 small firm tomatoes
7 oz tin tuna fish in brine (200 g)
8 small new potatoes, cooked and sliced
3 or 4 anchovies
12 black olives, stoned

1 tablespoon fresh parsley, chopped
1 onion, peeled and sliced

for the vinaigrette:
4–5 tablespoons olive oil
1 tablespoon white wine vinegar
½ teaspoon mustard powder
salt and freshly ground black pepper

Top and tail the French beans, cut them into one inch (2.5 cm) lengths, and cook for five minutes in lightly salted boiling water. Drain. Boil the eggs for ten minutes. Meanwhile, wash the lettuce leaves, spin or pat dry, and use to line a fairly large salad bowl. Slice the cucumber and cut the tomatoes into quarters. Drain and flake the tuna fish. When the eggs are ready, peel them and cut them into quarters. Gently mix the cucumber, tomatoes, beans, eggs, tuna, potatoes and olives and lightly pile the mixture into the salad bowl. Garnish with the anchovies, briefly soaked in milk to remove some of their saltiness, and the thinly sliced onions. Whisk the dressing ingredients together, drizzle over the salad just before serving, and sprinkle with the parsley.

SALMON MOUSSE

1 oz butter (25 g)
1 oz plain flour (25 g)
½ pint milk (275 ml)
salt and freshly ground black pepper
1 tablespoon fresh fennel or dill, chopped
2 inch piece cucumber, grated (5 cm)
8 oz tin salmon (225 g)
½ oz gelatine (15 g)
2 fresh eggs, separated

Melt the butter, stir in the flour and cook for one minute. Gradually stir in the milk, bring to the boil, and then add the dill or fennel together with some salt and pepper. Simmer for two minutes. Cool a little, then stir in the egg yolks, then the cucumber. Flake the salmon, discarding skin and bones but keeping the juices, and stir it in. Pour the juices from the tin into a small dish, bring the quantity up to about four tablespoons with cold water, and place this dish in a bowl of very hot water. Sprinkle the gelatine on the top and allow to dissolve. When the gelatine has completely dissolved, pour the liquid into the salmon mixture and stir. Leave in the fridge for about 30 minutes or until nearly set. Beat the egg whites until stiff, then fold into the salmon mixture and return to the fridge. You can either serve this from the bowl, or place it in little ramekin dishes, or, if you have them, scallop shells look pretty. Garnish with fronds of fresh dill or fennel.
Serves 4–6.

SMOKED MACKEREL AND DILL PATE

1 oz butter (25 g)
1 small onion, peeled and finely chopped
1 clove garlic, crushed
8 oz smoked mackerel (225 g)
1 egg, hard boiled and shelled
salt and freshly ground black pepper
3 tablespoons sour cream
1 tablespoon fresh dill, finely chopped

to serve:
fresh dill
1 lemon, quartered

Start by melting the butter and gently softening the onion and garlic. Meanwhile, flake the fish, discarding skin and bones. Mash it with the egg, then add the softened onion and garlic. Add the sour cream, salt and freshly ground black pepper, and the dill. Spoon into four ramekin dishes, and garnish with fronds of dill. Serve with thin hot toast and lemon quarters.

SMOKED SALMON NIBBLES

4 oz smoked salmon (110 g)
14 oz tin asparagus spears (400 g)
4 tablespoons good bought mayonnaise
salt and freshly ground black pepper
1 teaspoon dill weed
1 teaspoon lemon juice
6–8 slices brown bread
cocktail sticks

The quantities given are approximate, but you should be able to make 20–24 small rolls. Drain the asparagus spears and lay them on some kitchen paper and pat them as dry as possible. Cut the crusts off the bread and roll each slice with a rolling pin to stretch it and make it thinner. Beat together the mayonnaise, lemon juice, dill weed and some salt and pepper to taste. Cut each bread slice lengthways into three. Spread each strip with some of the mayonnaise mixture. Slice the salmon into thin pieces, and lay over the mayonnaise. Cut the asparagus into 1 inch (2.5 cm) lengths, and place on one end of each bread strip on top of the salmon. Roll up each strip carefully and spear to secure with a cocktail stick. If there is any salmon left over, cut very thinly, roll up and use to garnish the sticks; alternatively, use small stuffed green olives.

SPRING ROLLS

The advantage of making your own spring rolls is that you know exactly what good things have gone into them. You can serve these as starters, or as part of a Chinese meal.

2 sheets frozen filo pastry, defrosted
4 tablespoons sesame oil
8 oz shelled prawns or shrimps (225 g)
4 oz water chestnuts, drained and finely sliced (110 g)
2 oz mushrooms, wiped and sliced (55 g)
3 spring onions, finely chopped
$\frac{1}{2}$ inch piece root ginger, peeled and finely chopped (1.5 cm)
4 oz bean sprouts (110 g)
2 tablespoons medium dry sherry
2 tablespoons rich soy sauce
freshly ground black pepper
sunflower oil for frying

to garnish:
a few prawns or shrimps and some shredded spring onions

Heat the sesame oil in a large frying pan or wok and stir in the prawns or shrimps, water chestnuts, mushrooms, spring onions, root ginger, and beansprouts, and fry gently for about ten minutes, stirring all the time to prevent sticking. Pour in the sherry and soy sauce and add some black pepper. Remove from the heat.

Cut each piece of filo pastry into three strips, and divide the prawn mixture between the strips, placing about a tablespoonful on the end of each strip. Tuck in the sides of the pastry, then roll the strips up, not too tightly.

Heat the sunflower oil in a large frying pan and fry the six rolls gently for about eight minutes, turning frequently so that the rolls are golden on all sides. Serve hot, garnished with spring onions and prawns or shrimps.

Variations
Try using thinly sliced chicken instead of the prawns or shrimps; or you could make a vegetarian version with carrots, courgettes, beans, peas, and spinach, chopped or shredded finely.

STUFFED MUSHROOMS

4 large flat mushrooms, wiped clean
2 tablespoons corn or sunflower oil
1 medium onion, peeled and chopped
1 clove garlic, crushed and chopped
1 medium green pepper, deseeded and chopped
4 oz long grain brown rice (110 g)
1 pint chicken or vegetable stock (600 ml)
1 bay leaf, crushed
salt and freshly ground black pepper
2 oz hazelnuts, chopped (55 g)
2 oz farmhouse Cheddar, grated (55 g)

Heat the oil and soften the onion, garlic and pepper for a few minutes. Meanwhile, remove the stalks from the mushrooms, slice the stalks, and add to the pan. Stir, then add the rice, stock and bay leaf. Cover and simmer for 20 minutes or until the rice is cooked. Remove the bay leaf, add the hazelnuts and seasoning to taste, then pile the mixture into the four mushrooms. Put them on a greased baking tray, sprinkle with the cheese, and bake at Gas 4, 350 deg F, 180 deg C for 15–20 minutes or until brown and bubbling.

Note
This basic stuffing may also be used to stuff large beef tomatoes or green or red peppers. Tomatoes should be scooped out and their chopped flesh added to the rice as it cooks. Peppers need to have pith and seeds removed, should be blanched for five or ten minutes first, and will take slightly longer to bake.

STUFFED PLAICE FILLETS

2 fresh plaice fillets
1 tablespoon sunflower oil
1 small onion, peeled and finely chopped
5 oz cooked spinach (150 g)
2 oz pine nuts, roughly chopped (55 g)
juice of $\frac{1}{2}$ a lemon
$\frac{1}{4}$ teaspoon grated nutmeg
salt and freshly ground black pepper

Heat the oil in a small frying pan, then soften the onion. Meanwhile, mix together the spinach, pine nuts, half the lemon juice, nutmeg, and seasoning. Cut each plaice fillet in half lengthways, lay a tablespoon of the mixture down the middle and carefully roll up, starting from the wider end. Sprinkle on the remaining lemon juice, then lay the rolls in a buttered baking dish and cover with a lid or foil. Bake for 15 minutes at Gas 6, 400 deg F, 200 deg C. For a special occasion, whizz up a sauce with more cooked spinach, cream cheese, yogurt and seasoning.

VEGETABLE CRUDITES

Whet your guests' appetites with fresh young vegetables served with a good vinaigrette and a contrasting sauce.

> Seasonal vegetables, such as cooked beetroot, carrots, chicory, courgettes, cucumber, endive, fennel, peppers, radishes, and spring onions
> salt and freshly ground black pepper
> for the vinaigrette: 5–6 tablespoons olive oil
> 1 tablespoon white wine vinegar or lemon juice
> fresh herbs, such as parsley, tarragon, chives, thyme, chervil finely chopped
>
> for the dip:
> 1 ripe avocado, halved and stoned
> 4 oz cream cheese (110 g)
> 1 tablespoon lemon juice

Cut the chosen vegetables into tiny strips, or grate them. Do not mix them, but arrange in attractive wedges on individual plates. Make the vinaigrette dressing by shaking the olive oil with the lemon juice or vinegar and salt, pepper and fresh herbs to taste. Sprinkle a little vinaigrette dressing over the prepared vegetables. Mash the flesh of the avocado with the cream cheese and lemon juice, season, and place a dollop in the centre of each plate, surrounded by the vegetables.

WHISKY PRAWNS

> 1 oz butter (25 g)
> 1 small onion, peeled and finely chopped
> 1 tablespoon plain flour
> $\frac{1}{4}$ pint milk (150 ml)
> $\frac{1}{4}$ pint double cream (150 ml)
> 2 fl oz whisky (55 ml)
> 4 oz peeled prawns (110 g)
>
> to garnish:
> paprika

Melt the butter in a small pan, then gently soften the onion. When it is transparent, stir in the flour and cook for one minute. Now add the milk little by little, then the cream, and simmer until the sauce thickens. Stir in the whisky and prawns, and heat through for a couple of minutes. Serve piping hot, garnished with paprika, and accompanied by thin slices of brown bread.
Serves 2–3.

SOUPS

Cauliflower · Parsnip · Chicken · Tomato · Beans · Nettle · Pea

SOUPS

Some people never make soup at home, and it's not surprising when many cookery books tell you to boil up huge quantities of bones and other remnants before you can even start.

For some soups, this may still be necessary, but you won't find them listed here. Most soups work well with a decent stock cube, or even with frozen stock from supermarkets. The one exception is fish stock, which I think is worth making, because it only takes a few minutes to boil up bones and skin with a little lemon juice and it tastes a lot better than any commercial stock I've come across.

Once you've got the hang of soup making, you can make any kind that takes your fancy, out of whatever ingredients you like. You can leave it chunky, or liquidise it, or make it posh enough to serve at a dinner party by swirling in cream and sprinkling with snipped chives or paprika or croutons.

You can make a soup thick enough to stand your spoon up in, which, full of beans and pulses, and served with loads of warm bread, will feed a hungry family and be a lot cheaper than a meat casserole.

Bean and pasta
Beetroot
Broad bean
Carrot and cauliflower
Celery and Stilton
Chinese chicken and mushroom
Courgette and nettle
Creamy potato
Cucumber
Curried parsnip
Fennel
Fish
French onion

Gazpacho (iced Spanish tomato soup)
Ham, leek and pea
Jerusalem artichoke
Lamb and lentil
Leek and potato
Lentil
Lettuce and watercress
Minestrone
Mushroom and rosemary
Pasta and bean
Red bean chilli
Tomato and basil
Turkey and red bean

BEAN SOUP

6 oz mixed dried beans (175 g)
2 tablespoons sunflower oil
1 large onion, peeled and chopped
1 carrot, scrubbed and chopped
the white of a leek, washed and sliced
2 cloves garlic, peeled and crushed
approx 2 pints beef stock (1.2 litres)
2 tablespoons tomato purée
salt and freshly ground black pepper
2 teaspoons Marmite
4 oz small pasta shapes (110 g)

to garnish:
1 tablespoon fresh parsley, chopped

Wash the beans and soak them overnight in plenty of cold water. Next day, heat the oil in a large saucepan or flameproof casserole and soften the onion. Add the carrot, leek and garlic and cook gently for five to ten minutes, stirring now and then. Drain the soaked beans and add them to the vegetables in the pan together with the tomato purée, Marmite, and some seasoning, and pour in the stock. Bring to the boil, skim, turn down the heat, cover and simmer for an hour or so; add the pasta ten minutes before the end of the cooking time, and allow to cook until soft but not mushy. Check the seasoning, then serve the soup very hot sprinkled with the parsley. Serve with wholemeal bread.
Serves 4–6.

BEETROOT SOUP

1 oz butter (25 g)
1 onion, peeled and chopped
2 sticks celery, scrubbed and chopped
1 lb beetroot, cooked and skinned (450 g)
$1\frac{1}{2}$ pints chicken stock (900 ml)
a sprig of fresh thyme
salt and freshly ground black pepper
$\frac{1}{4}$ pint sour cream (150 ml)

to garnish:
1 tablespoon chives, snipped

Melt the butter in a flameproof casserole and soften the onion and celery for five to ten minutes, making sure they do not brown. Slice or chop the beetroot into fairly large pieces, and add to the casserole together with the chicken stock, thyme and seasoning. Bring to the boil, then turn down the heat and simmer, covered, for about half an hour, or until the celery is tender. Sieve or liquidise the contents of the pan, check the seasoning and reheat gently. Spoon into warmed soup bowls and swirl in the soured cream. Garnish with snipped chives.
Serves 4–6.

BROAD BEAN SOUP

2 lb young broad beans (unshelled weight) (1 kg)
4 oz peas, fresh or frozen (shelled weight) (110 g)
1¾ pints vegetable stock (1 litre)
2 rashers unsmoked bacon, chopped small
1 tablespoon olive oil
1 clove garlic, peeled and crushed
1 tablespoon plain flour
salt and freshly ground black pepper
2 tablespoons fresh parsley, chopped

Shell the broad beans and then remove the coarse outer skin from each bean (this is fiddly but well worth doing). Simmer the beans and peas in the vegetable stock for five minutes. Meanwhile, heat the oil gently in a small frying pan and then soften the garlic and bacon. Stir in the flour and cook for one minute, then stir the contents of the frying pan into the saucepan with the peas and beans. The soup will thicken slightly, but it's not meant to be very thick. Season, and cook for another couple of minutes. Pour into warmed soup bowls, sprinkle liberally with parsley, and serve with wholemeal bread.
Serves 3–4.

CARROT AND CAULIFLOWER SOUP

1 large cauliflower, washed and divided into florets
8 oz carrots, scrubbed and chopped (225 g)
¾ pint chicken or vegetable stock (425 ml)
a sprig each of thyme and rosemary
2 sage leaves
1 oz butter (25 g)
1 oz flour (25 g)
½ pint milk (300 ml)
¼ pint double cream (150 ml) (optional)

Cook the carrots and cauliflower in the stock together with the herbs for about 20 minutes or until the vegetables are tender. While they are cooking, melt the butter in a small pan and stir in the flour to make a smooth paste. Cook for one minute, stirring to prevent sticking and burning, then add the milk little by little, stirring all the time until you have a smooth, thick sauce. Liquidise or blend this sauce with the drained vegetables and ½ pint (300 ml) of the stock in which the vegetables were cooked. Discard the herbs. Return the liquidised vegetables to the pan and thin if necessary with the rest of the vegetable stock. Season with salt and freshly ground black pepper. Serve hot. Swirl in the cream just before serving, if using.
Serves 4–6.

CELERY AND STILTON SOUP

1 oz butter (25 g)
1 tablespoon corn or sunflower oil
6 celery sticks, wiped, trimmed and chopped
3 tablespoons flour
½ pint milk (300 ml)
1 pint chicken stock (600 ml)
8 oz ripe Stilton cheese, grated or crumbled (225 g)
salt and freshly ground black pepper

to garnish:
1 tablespoon fresh lovage leaves, chopped (optional)

Melt the butter and oil together in a saucepan, then add the celery and cook gently for 5–10 minutes, until softened but not browned. Add the flour, and cook gently for one minute, stirring all the time. Over a gentle heat, gradually add the milk and chicken stock, stir well until smooth, then bring to the boil. Turn down the heat, cover, and simmer for 15 minutes, or until the celery is tender. Add the Stilton little by little, stirring well until it has melted. Season with salt and pepper, heat through, and serve hot, sprinkled with lovage if using.

CHINESE CHICKEN AND MUSHROOM SOUP

the neck and wings of a fresh chicken
2 pints water (1.2 litres)
1 small onion, peeled and quartered
1 carrot, scrubbed and roughly chopped
1 bay leaf, crushed
1 sprig thyme
a few parsley sprigs
1 tablespoon rich soy sauce
salt and freshly ground white pepper
4 button mushrooms, wiped
the white of a small leek, washed

Place the chicken pieces, water, onion, carrot, and herbs in a large saucepan. Bring to the boil, skim, then turn down the heat, cover, and simmer for an hour and a half. Strain, discard the chicken and vegetables, and return the clear stock to the pan (wash it first to remove any bits clinging to the sides of the pan.) Season with the soy sauce, and some salt and freshly ground white pepper. Slice the mushrooms and leek as thinly as you possibly can, then add to the soup. Heat through for five minutes without boiling, then serve at once.

COURGETTE AND NETTLE SOUP

6 oz young nettle tops and leaves (175 g)
2 tablespoons sunflower oil
2 small courgettes, sliced
1 large onion, peeled and chopped
1 large potato, peeled and chopped
1 tablespoon fresh parsley or tarragon
2 pints chicken or vegetable stock (1.2 litres)
salt and freshly ground black pepper
3 tablespoons double cream

Heat the oil in a large saucepan and sauté the courgettes, onion and potato for about ten minutes, stirring now and then. When they are soft, add the nettle leaves and herbs, stir well, and then pour in the stock. Bring to the boil, then reduce to a simmer. Season lightly, cover, and cook gently for 20 minutes, stirring from time to time. Sieve or liquidise, return to the saucepan and reheat gently. Check the seasoning, and serve with a generous swirl of cream.
Serves 4–6.

CREAMY POTATO SOUP

This creamy soup is simple and cheap to make, but delicious to eat and particularly warming on a cold winter's night. A few fresh herbs, parsley, chives, or whatever you can find, make all the difference.

½ oz butter (15 g)
1 lb potatoes, peeled and sliced (450 g)
1 medium onion, peeled and sliced
½ oz plain flour (15 g)
1 pint chicken stock (600 ml)
2 fl oz single cream (55 ml)
salt and freshly ground black pepper

to garnish:
fresh parsley, chopped, or fresh chives, snipped

Melt the butter in a large saucepan, then add the onions and potatoes. Let them soften slightly for a few minutes, without browning. Stir in the flour, cook for a minute, then add the stock and a little salt. Bring to the boil, then turn down the heat, cover the pan and simmer until the vegetables are tender. Liquidise or sieve. Return to the pan, add the cream, a little more salt if needed, some freshly ground black pepper, and warm through very gently. Thin with a little chicken stock, milk, or water if necessary. Sprinkle with chopped parsley or snipped chives before serving.

CUCUMBER SOUP

1 cucumber, thinly sliced
2 oz butter (55 g)
1 pint vegetable stock (600 ml)
3 tablespoons fresh parsley, finely chopped
¼ pint milk (150 ml)
2 egg yolks
salt and freshly ground white pepper
1 lemon, quartered

Melt the butter in a heavy-based pan, then tip in the sliced cucumber and allow it to sweat gently for five minutes. Add the vegetable stock and parsley, season, and cook gently for another ten minutes, stirring now and then. Beat the egg yolks and milk together, and then gradually pour into the soup. Do this over a very gentle heat or the eggs will curdle and the whole thing will look revolting. Season. Serve the soup hot, and give everyone a lemon quarter to squeeze into his or her bowl.

CURRIED PARSNIP SOUP

This creamy, faintly spicy, soup is based on one devised by Jane Grigson, whose cookbooks are a joy to read as well as to cook from.

3 oz butter (75 g)
1 large parsnip, scrubbed or peeled and diced
1 medium onion, peeled and diced
1 clove garlic, peeled and crushed
1 tablespoon flour
1 rounded teaspoon curry powder
2 pints hot beef stock (1.2 litres)
salt and freshly ground black pepper
¼ pint double cream (150 ml)
1 tablespoon fresh coriander or chives, chopped or snipped

Melt the butter in a large pan, then add the parsnip, onion and garlic. Cover and cook very gently for ten minutes, stirring now and then. The vegetables must not brown, only absorb the butter. Sprinkle in the flour and curry powder, stir around to take up the fat, and cook for one minute. Gradually add the hot beef stock, then simmer, covered, until the parsnip is cooked. Liquidise. Return to the pan; add salt, pepper and a little more curry powder if necessary (but remember that the flavour is supposed to be mild.) Stir in the cream and heat through; sprinkle with coriander or chives before serving. Serve hot, with croutons of bread fried in butter and oil. Serves 6–8.

FENNEL SOUP

Fennel has a strong aniseed aroma when eaten raw and many people don't like it. However, cooked, as in this soup, the scent is much milder and the taste is really delicious.

3 oz butter (75 g)
1 large bulb fennel, trimmed and sliced
1 onion, peeled and sliced
2 potatoes, peeled and chopped
2 pints chicken stock (1.2 litres)
1½ tablespoons plain flour
¼ pint double cream (150 ml)
salt and freshly ground black pepper

to garnish:
fresh fennel

Melt the butter in a heavy-bottomed pan and gently soften all the vegetables for about 10 minutes, stirring frequently so they all get coated in the butter. Pour in the stock, add a little salt, bring to the boil, cover, and simmer for about half an hour or until the vegetables are tender. Sieve or liquidise. Return to the pan, add the cream, more salt if needed, and some pepper. Reheat very gently. Garnish with fronds of fennel, either taken from the bulb, or from your herb bed in the garden, if you have one.
Serves 6–8.

FISH SOUP

the white of a leek, washed and chopped
1 onion, peeled and chopped
1 carrot, scrubbed and chopped
2 cloves garlic, peeled and crushed
2 tablespoons oil
14 oz tin tomatoes (400 g)
½ pint dry white wine (300 ml)

1½ pints fish stock (900 ml)
12 oz fresh cod, haddock, or coley (350 g)
4 oz fresh shrimps or prawns (110 g)
2 scallops, thinly sliced
12 mussels, cleaned
2 tablespoons fresh parsley, chopped
freshly ground black pepper

Heat the oil in a large saucepan and soften the leek, onion, carrot and garlic. Add the tomatoes and their juice, wine, and some pepper and simmer for 20 minutes. Now add the fish stock and parsley, and boil for 2 or 3 minutes. Cut the fish into bite-sized chunks and add to the soup. Turn down the heat and cook gently for a further 10 minutes, then add the shrimps or prawns and the scallops, and heat through. While the fish is cooking, you should cook the mussels separately for a few minutes in a little hot white wine or water, discarding any that do not open. Shell them and add them to the soup just before serving. Strain the mussels' cooking liquor, and add that to the soup.

FRENCH ONION SOUP

$1\frac{1}{2}$ lb onions (675 g)
2 oz butter (55 g)
1 teaspoon sugar
1 oz plain flour (25 g)
2 pints hot beef stock (1.2 litres)
$\frac{1}{2}$ inch slices of French bread (2.5 cm)
2 oz farmhouse Cheddar, roughly grated (55 g)
salt and freshly ground black pepper
1 tablespoon sweet sherry or brandy

Peel and thinly slice the onions. Melt the butter in a fairly large pan and gently cook the onions until they are softened. Add the sugar, and continue cooking, stirring now and then, until the onions are golden brown. Now add the flour, cook for one minute, then add the stock. Season. Cover and simmer gently for an hour, stirring occasionally. Toast the bread lightly on both sides, put it into flameproof soup bowls, pour the soup into the bowls, and add a splash of sherry or brandy. When the French bread rises to the surface, cover it liberally with the grated cheese, and brown under the grill. Serve immediately.

GAZPACHO
Iced Spanish tomato soup

1 lb ripe tomatoes (450 g)
2 inch piece of cucumber, chopped (5 cm)
$\frac{1}{2}$ a red pepper, deseeded and chopped
$\frac{1}{2}$ a green pepper, deseeded and chopped
2 cloves garlic, peeled and crushed
1 red onion, peeled and chopped
1 pint tomato juice (570 ml)
1 teaspoon Worcester sauce
juice of $\frac{1}{2}$ a lemon
1 tablespoon fresh herbs, chopped
salt and freshly ground black pepper

to serve:
ice cubes and croutons

Try to obtain tomatoes with real flavour for this soup; the best ones come from Provence—they cost more, but it's worth it. Otherwise, make sure the tomatoes are really ripe. Remove their skins by plunging them into boiling water and leaving for a few minutes, after which time the skins should peel off easily. Discard the skins, remove pips if possible, and chop the tomatoes roughly. Keep back a tablespoon each of the diced cucumber, peppers, and onion, then put all the other main ingredients in a liquidiser, and whizz them up together until completely smooth. Check the seasoning. Pour the soup into a pretty glass serving bowl, and chill until needed. Add 10 ice cubes just before serving, and offer with the reserved vegetables and some croutons fried in butter and oil for everyone to make a personal selection. Serves 4–6.

HAM, LEEK AND PEA SOUP

1 pork knuckle or hock
3 leeks, washed
1 carrot, scrubbed and chopped roughly
1 onion, peeled and chopped
1 bay leaf, crushed
1 tablespoon parsley stalks
4–6 sage leaves
4 oz split peas (110 g)
1 oz butter (25 g)
salt and freshly ground black pepper

Place the knuckle or hock with the carrot, onion, and herbs in a saucepan with 2 pints (1.2 litres) of water. Chop the green parts of the leeks and add to the pan. Bring to the boil, skim, cover, and simmer for two hours. Drain, reserving the liquid. Take off any meat from the bone and chop it small, then discard the fat, bones and the contents of the sieve. When the stock has cooled, skim the fat from the surface. Cover the split peas with water, boil for 10 minutes, then simmer, covered, for 30 minutes. Add the peas to the stock with enough of their water to bring it up to about 2 pints (1.2 litres.) Bring to the boil, then simmer for 10–15 minutes. Chop the reserved whites of leeks small. Melt the butter in a small frying pan, and saute the chopped leeks. When they are soft, add them to the soup. Season. Serve hot with crusty rolls.

JERUSALEM ARTICHOKE SOUP

1 lb Jerusalem artichokes, peeled (450 g)
$1\frac{1}{4}$ pints chicken or vegetable stock (750 ml)
1 teaspoon fresh basil, chopped, or $\frac{1}{2}$ teaspoon dried basil
1 bay leaf, crushed
3–4 sprigs parsley
1 onion, peeled and chopped roughly
1 oz butter (25 g)
1 oz plain flour (25 g)
$\frac{1}{2}$ pint milk (300 ml)
$\frac{1}{4}$ pint single cream (150 ml)
salt and freshly ground black pepper

to serve:
fresh parsley, chopped

Cut the peeled artichokes fairly small. Put them in a pan with the stock, herbs and onion. Bring to the boil, turn down the heat, cover, and simmer for about 45 minutes or until tender. Strain, and remove the bay leaf and parsley. Reserve the cooking liquor. Liquidise or sieve the vegetables. Heat the butter in the pan, blend in the flour and cook for one minute. Add the reserved cooking liquor, milk, artichoke purée and some salt and pepper, and bring to the boil. Turn down the heat, simmer for five minutes, then add the cream and gently heat through. Serve sprinkled with fresh chopped parsley.

LAMB AND LENTIL SOUP

8 oz (approx) lean cooked lamb (225 g)
1 large onion, peeled and chopped finely
2 leeks, washed and shredded
4 medium carrots, scrubbed and chopped
14 oz tin tomatoes and their juice (400 g)
4 oz red lentils (110 g)
a handful of fresh herbs, or 2 teaspoons mixed dried herbs
salt and freshly ground black pepper
dash of Worcester or soy sauce

Cut all the meat into small pieces, discarding any fat. Place meat, lamb bones, if you have any, and all the other ingredients in a large saucepan, cover with water, bring to the boil, skim and then turn down the heat. Cover, and simmer gently for two or three hours. Remove the bones, if using, before serving. Serve piping hot with plenty of wholemeal bread.
Serves 4–6.

LEEK AND POTATO SOUP

1½ lb leeks, whites only, washed and shredded (700 g)
2 medium onions, peeled and chopped
2 oz butter (55 g)
1 clove garlic, peeled and crushed
1 lb potatoes, peeled and diced (450 g)
2 pints hot chicken stock (1.2 litres)
salt and freshly ground black pepper

to garnish:
1 tablespoon fresh parsley, chopped,
or 1 tablespoon fresh chives, snipped

Melt the butter in a heavy-bottomed saucepan and add the leeks, garlic and onion. Cover and sweat gently for ten minutes. Stir in the potatoes, cover, and cook gently for a further ten minutes. Stir in the hot stock and simmer, covered, for 30–40 minutes, or until the vegetables are quite tender. Add seasoning to taste, then sieve or liquidise. Reheat gently, check the seasoning, pour into warmed bowls and garnish with parsley or chives.

LENTIL SOUP

6 oz red lentils (175 g)
1½ pints hot chicken stock (850 ml)
1 onion, peeled and chopped
4 celery stalks, scrubbed and chopped
2 carrots, scrubbed and chopped
14 oz tin tomatoes and their juice (400 g)
1 bay leaf, crushed
salt and freshly ground black pepper

to garnish:
celery leaves, chopped

Place all the ingredients in a large pan and bring to the boil. Skim, then cover, turn down the heat, and simmer gently for 40–50 minutes, until the vegetables are all tender. Remove the bay leaf, then sieve or liquidise, and return to the pan. Check the seasoning and reheat gently. Garnish with chopped celery leaves before serving.

Variations
This soup is also good if you add a teaspoon of spices (turmeric, cumin and ginger; or curry powder) before liquidising. Or, if you like a rough-textured, country-style soup, you do not have to liquidise this one; only make sure you chop the vegetables evenly, and mash the tomatoes well before adding.

LETTUCE AND WATERCRESS SOUP

1 oz butter (25 g)
1 small onion, peeled and chopped
1 clove garlic, peeled and crushed
1 large or two small lettuces, trimmed and washed
1 bunch watercress, washed and toughest stalks removed
1 tablespoon each parsley and mint, chopped small
1 sprig thyme
¾ pint water or vegetable stock (425 ml)
salt and freshly ground black pepper

to serve:
croutons fried in butter and olive oil

Heat the butter in a large saucepan and soften the onion and garlic. Meanwhile, shred the lettuce and watercress, then add them to the pan, stir well, cover and cook gently for another five minutes. Add the herbs, water or stock, and some salt and pepper. Simmer very gently for 15–20 minutes, then remove the thyme and sieve or liquidise. Reheat gently and serve immediately, with croutons.

MINESTRONE

A proper minestrone is a meal in itself, and recipes vary according to which part of Italy they come from. This is a good basic recipe which can be varied according to vegetables in season.

>1 oz butter (25 g)
>2 rashers streaky bacon, finely chopped
>2 small leeks, whites only, washed and shredded
>1 large onion, peeled and finely chopped
>1 clove garlic, peeled and crushed
>2 carrots, scrubbed and diced
>1 small turnip, scrubbed and chopped
>2 sticks celery, scrubbed and chopped
>2 pints hot beef stock (1.2 litres)
>1 teaspoon mixed dried herbs, or a handful of parsley stalks, sprigs of thyme and rosemary, and a few sage leaves
>4 oz shortcut macaroni (110 g)
>8 oz tin chopped tomatoes and their juice (225 g)
>1 dessertspoon tomato purée
>salt and freshly ground black pepper
>4 oz cabbage, washed and finely shredded (110 g)
>
>to serve:
>plenty of freshly grated Parmesan cheese

Melt the butter in a large heavy-bottomed casserole, then fry the bacon until the fat runs. Add the leeks, onion and garlic, and cook for five to ten minutes until the onion is soft. Add the carrots, turnip and celery, and stir well. Add the stock and herbs and bring to the boil. Cover, and simmer for 20–30 minutes.

Add the macaroni and tomatoes and their juices, and simmer for another 20 minutes. Stir in the tomato purée and season with salt and freshly ground black pepper. Cook for another ten minutes. In another pan, boil the chopped cabbage for five minutes, then drain well. Divide between large warmed soup bowls.

Remove the fresh herbs from the soup, and discard. Pour the piping hot soup over the cabbage. Serve the grated Parmesan at the table to allow people to help themselves.
Serves 6.

MUSHROOM AND ROSEMARY SOUP

Rosemary goes surprisingly well with mushrooms, although I do think you need to use the fresh herb rather than the dried, which tends to be rather spiky and powdery in taste as well as texture.

> 10 oz mushrooms, wiped and roughly chopped (275 g)
> 2 oz butter (55 g)
> 1 oz flour (25 g)
> ¾ pint vegetable stock (425 ml)
> ¾ pint milk (425 ml)
> 2 or 3 sprigs fresh rosemary
> ½ teaspoon freshly grated nutmeg
> salt and freshly ground black pepper
> 2–3 tablespoons red wine

Melt the butter in a heavy-based saucepan and sauté the mushrooms in it for about 15 minutes. Stir in the flour, then gradually add the vegetable stock and the milk. Add the rosemary, and season with nutmeg, salt and pepper. Simmer for another 15 minutes. Just before serving, remove the rosemary, stir in the red wine and heat through without boiling. Serve at once.

PASTA AND BEAN SOUP

> 4 oz broad beans (shelled weight) (110 g)
> 1 large onion, peeled and sliced
> 2 pints hot beef or vegetable stock (1.2 litres)
> 14 oz can red kidney beans, drained and rinsed (400 g)
> 3 oz wholemeal pasta bows or shells (75 g)
> 1 tablespoon tomato purée
> 1 bay leaf, crushed
> salt and freshly ground black pepper

to garnish:
> 1 tablespoon fresh parsley, chopped

Place the broad beans and onion in a large saucepan. Pour on the hot stock, cover, and simmer for about ten minutes. Add the kidney beans, pasta, tomato purée, bay leaf and seasoning, turn up the heat a little, cover, and cook for 10–15 minutes or until the pasta is tender. Remove the bay leaf and serve piping hot, with the parsley sprinkled on top.

RED BEAN CHILLI SOUP

1–2 tablespoons corn or sunflower oil
2 onions, peeled and coarsely chopped
1 clove garlic, crushed
1 level teaspoon chilli powder
14 oz tin Italian tomatoes, chopped, and their juice (400 g)
½ pint beef stock (300 ml)
14 oz tin red kidney beans, drained (400 g)
salt and freshly ground black pepper

Heat the oil in a large heavy-bottomed saucepan and then gently fry the onions and garlic. Continue cooking until they are soft and golden, then stir in the chilli powder. Cook, stirring, for a couple of minutes, then add the tomatoes and their juice, and the beef stock. Bring to the boil, turn down the heat, and add the red kidney beans. Add seasoning to taste. Heat through for five to ten minutes, then serve with crusty bread.
Serves 4–6.

TOMATO AND BASIL SOUP

Basil is one of my favourite herbs. It's very easy to grow and has a natural affinity with tomatoes; if you grow some next to your tomatoes in the garden, it will keep pests at bay. And then it's easy to pick the two together, for salads or this lovely soup!

2 oz butter (55 g)
2 onions, peeled and chopped
1 clove garlic, crushed
2 lb tomatoes (1 kg)
3 tablespoons flour
1½ pint chicken stock (900 ml)
2 tablespoons tomato purée
1 tablespoon fresh basil, chopped
salt and freshly ground black pepper
¼ pint single cream (150 ml) (optional)

Melt the butter, then soften the onions and garlic. Meanwhile, wash or wipe the tomatoes and cut them in half. Scoop out the seeds, place them in a sieve and press down to release the juice. Sprinkle the flour into the pan with the onions and cook gently for one minute, then add the stock little by little. Bring to the boil slowly, and keep stirring until thickened. Stir in the tomatoes, their reserved juices, tomato purée and basil, and season with salt and pepper. Cover and simmer gently for 30 minutes. Allow to cool a little, then sieve or liquidise, strain through a sieve into a clean pan and reheat gently. Check the seasoning. Ladle into warmed soup bowls and finish off with a swirl of cream, if using, in each bowl.
Serves 6.

TURKEY AND RED BEAN SOUP

1 cooked turkey carcass including bones, skin, giblets, etc
2 tablespoons fresh herbs or 1 tablespoon mixed dried herbs
8–12 oz leftover cooked turkey (225–350 g)
1 tablespoon sunflower oil
1 carrot, scrubbed and chopped
1 onion, peeled and chopped
14 oz can red kidney beans (400 g)
1 tablespoon tomato purée
salt and freshly ground black pepper

Place the turkey carcass and remains in a large pan together with the herbs and about 3 pints (1.8 litres) of water. Bring to the boil, skim, then simmer for 40 minutes. Strain, discard the carcass and odds and ends, and boil the liquid you have left down to 2 pints (1.2 litres.) Now heat the oil in a large pan and gently soften the onion and carrot. Add the strained stock, tomato purée, cold turkey meat and the red beans. Season with quite liberally with salt and pepper and simmer for 15 minutes. Serve hot.

VEGETABLE SOUP WITH DUMPLINGS

2 oz butter (55 g)
1 onion, peeled and finely chopped
1 clove garlic, crushed
1 small turnip, scrubbed and diced
2 carrots, scrubbed and diced
2 pints beef stock (1.2 litres)

for the dumplings:
3 slices from a white loaf
3 small pork sausages
1 tablespoon each finely chopped parsley and sage
  (or 2 teaspoons mixed dried herbs)
salt and freshly ground black pepper
the heart of a spring cabbage

Melt half the butter in a large pan and gently soften the onion and garlic. Now add the diced turnip and carrots, cover, and cook very gently for five to ten minutes. Add the stock, bring to the boil, then simmer for ten minutes. Meanwhile, make the dumplings. Cut the crusts off the bread, dip the slices briefly in water, then squeeze out. Remove the skins from the sausages and combine the sausagemeat, bread, herbs, salt and freshly ground black pepper. Form into eight to ten small round dumplings and then drop them into the soup. Turn up the heat a little and continue cooking for 10–15 minutes. Chop the spring greens finely and boil for five minutes until just cooked. Melt the remaining butter and toss the spring greens in it. Place the greens in the bottom of two or four soup bowls, and pour the hot soup and dumplings over the top.
Serves 3–4.

FISH

Red Mullet · Mackerel · Sea bream · Trout · Salmon · Skate

FISH

The good news is that fish is a healthy option and we are eating more of it. Supermarkets are generally stocking more fish than they used to, and it is quick and easy to cook.

The bad news is that we tend to buy popular, well-known varieties like cod and haddock, and ignore species we haven't tried, even though the popular varieties are really quite expensive.

So give the cod and haddock population a chance, and experiment with different fish. And instead of simply frying or grilling, try alternative cooking methods. You can't really go wrong; if you overcook it, it will be dry or fall to bits, but, unlike meat, fish is never tough, gristly, stringy or chewy!

Fresh fish is always best if you can get it, and if it really is fresh. If you are not confident of how fresh it is (it should be firm, moist but not slimy, and most definitely not smell fishy) you are better off buying frozen fish, which is of a much better quality than it used to be.

The fish in many of these recipes is interchangeable; so that you could, for example, use plaice instead of brill, haddock instead of hake, and so on. But I do think that the tuna in red wine and herbs is a particularly flavoursome combination, and sea bream with apple is one of my favourite fish dishes.

Baked red mullet
Baked monkfish
Brill à la fermière
Cod and broccoli bake
Cod Provençale
Cold poached salmon with watercress sauce
Fish and mushroom pie
Fish cakes
Fish chowder
Haddock with mushrooms
Hake and potato bake
Hake in white wine
Italian seafood risotto

Mackerel in cider
Mackerel with herbs
Paella (shellfish, chicken and rice)
Prawn, spinach and mushroom pie
Salmon en croûte
Sea bream with apple
Sea bream meunière
Seafood thermidor
Skate baked with green olives
Skate with black butter
Somerset fish
Spicy fish
Tuna baked in red wine and herbs
Trout with herbs and lemon

BAKED RED MULLET

for each person, you need:
1 red mullet, weighing about 6 oz (150 g)
½ oz butter (15 g)
1 teaspoon fresh lemon juice
salt and freshly ground black pepper
1 teaspoon parsley, chopped
greaseproof paper

Descale and decapitate the fish if this has not already been done by the fishmonger. Remove the insides, leaving the liver in if you can identify it. Rinse the fish and pat dry. Place each fish on a separate sheet of buttered greaseproof paper, and dot with butter. Sprinkle the lemon juice, herbs and a little salt and pepper on top. Fold the paper carefully around the fish, pleating it on top and allowing enough room for the air to expand. Place the parcels in a baking dish and bake for 30 minutes at Gas 6, 400 deg F, 200 deg C. Served with a steamed green vegetable and small new potatoes.

BAKED MONKFISH

1 onion, peeled and chopped
1 stick celery, scrubbed and chopped
1 carrot, scrubbed and chopped
juice and zest of ½ a lemon
1 tablespoon fresh parsley
1 sprig of thyme
1 bay leaf, crushed
¾ pint water (450 ml)
6 peppercorns
¼ pint dry white wine (150 ml)
a little butter
8 small or 4 large monkfish steaks
¼ pint double cream (150 ml)

Scrub or peel the vegetables and chop them roughly. Put them in a saucepan with the lemon zest and juice, herbs, water and peppercorns and simmer for about an hour. Strain, keeping the stock and discarding the vegetables, etc. Place the fish in a shallow, lightly buttered dish and pour in the wine and enough stock to cover. Cover the dish with a lid or buttered foil and bake in the oven for 45–50 minutes at Gas 5, 375 deg F, 190 deg C. If the fish is cooked, it will be opaque and will come easily away from the central bone. Remove the fish and keep it warm on a serving dish. Pour the stock into a saucepan and reduce by half by boiling rapidly. Turn down the heat, add the cream, heat through very gently, and check the seasoning. Pour over the fish and serve at once.

BRILL A LA FERMIERE

The title means "farmer's wife brill", and I suppose the combination of vegetables is what a French countrywoman would have had to hand. But it was actually my husband who found and adapted this recipe, and the result is ... Brill!

> *1 brill, weighing about 2 lbs (1 kg)*
> *2 carrots, scrubbed and chopped*
> *1 large onion, peeled and sliced*
> *2 leeks (whites only), cleaned and sliced*
> *3 stalks celery, scrubbed and chopped*
> *2 oz butter (55 g)*
> *4 tablespoons dry white wine*
> *2 tablespoons double cream*
> *salt and freshly ground black pepper*

Melt the butter, thinly slice the vegetables, and sweat them slowly in the butter for 15–20 minutes. Meanwhile, grease an oval ovenproof dish large enough to take the fish, and clean and season the fish. Place half the vegetables in the bottom of the dish, place the brill on top, and arrange the rest of the vegetables over the top. Pour in the wine, cover and cook at Gas 6, 400 deg F, 200 deg C, basting occasionally. The fish will take 30–40 minutes to cook depending on size; if a knife slides through the flesh easily and it is quite opaque, it is ready. Drain off the cooking liquid into a saucepan, reduce by boiling to about half, take off the heat, stir in the cream, heat through gently, and pour over the fish.
Serves 3–4.

COD AND BROCCOLI BAKE

> *1 lb cod fillets or steaks (450 g)*
> *1 lb broccoli spears (450 g)*
> *1 pint milk (600 ml)*
> *2 oz butter (55 g)*
> *1½ oz flour (40 g)*
> *2 oz farmhouse Cheddar, grated (55 g)*
> *½ teaspoon freshly grated nutmeg*
> *salt and freshly ground black pepper*

Poach the fish very gently in the milk for about ten minutes. Reserve the milk, remove the fish, take off any skin, and flake into large chunks. Place in a large, shallow ovenproof dish and keep warm. While the fish is cooking, steam or boil the broccoli until just cooked. Drain it and arrange in with the fish. Melt the butter, stir in the flour, cook for one minute, then add the milk little by little, stirring well until you have a smooth sauce. Stir in the cheese, salt, pepper and nutmeg. When the cheese has melted, pour the sauce over the fish and broccoli, cover and bake in the oven for 30 minutes at Gas 4, 350 deg F, 180 deg C.

COD PROVENCALE

Cod on a ratatouille base is a summertime favourite in our house. You can use any white fish, and vary the vegetables according to what is in season.

 2 tablespoons olive oil
 1 large onion, peeled and chopped
 1 clove garlic, crushed
 1 small red pepper, deseeded and chopped
 1 aubergine, sliced
 2 courgettes, sliced
 14 oz tin tomatoes (400 g)
 1 sprig thyme
 1 bay leaf
 4 thick cod steaks
 3 tablespoons fresh breadcrumbs
 1 tablespoon farmhouse Cheddar, grated
 salt and freshly ground black pepper

Heat the oil, then soften the onion and garlic. When the onion is transparent, stir in the pepper, aubergine, courgettes, tomatoes and their juices, and herbs. Season, stir well, then cover and simmer gently for about an hour, stirring now and then. When the ratatouille mixture is soft, pour it into the base of a shallow baking dish and lay the cod steaks over it. Sprinkle the breadcrumbs and cheese on top, cover, and bake for 30 minutes at Gas 6, 400 deg F, 200 deg C. Uncover during the last five minutes to allow the topping to crisp up. Serve with crusty French bread.

COLD POACHED SALMON WITH WATERCRESS SAUCE

Many people think that salmon, being a meaty-looking fish, needs the same amount of cooking time as meat. This is not the case. The method given below for poaching the salmon is the best way to cook it if you wish to serve it cold. The method is quick, simple and effective, and the fish is guaranteed to be firm, sweet and moist.

> *4 salmon steaks*
> *1 small bunch fresh chives, snipped*
> *1 small bunch fresh parsley, chopped*
> *1 bunch watercress*
> *½ pint mayonnaise (300 ml)*
>
> to garnish:
> *watercress and lemon quarters*

Place the salmon in a deep frying pan, cover with cold water, bring to the boil, cover with a lid, boil for five seconds, then remove the pan from the heat and allow the fish to get quite cold in the water. When the salmon is cold, it will be cooked, and may be removed from the pan.

To make the sauce: blanch the watercress and herbs in boiling water for one minute, then chop as small as possible. Make the mayonnaise by beating the egg yolks with the salt and pepper and then beating in the olive oil drop by drop. It takes time to begin with, then later on you can add the olive oil in greater quantities. Now add the chopped herbs and watercress, beating until the sauce is smooth and velvety. Do not mix the herbs into the mayonnaise until shortly before serving, or the lovely green colour will fade. Serve the salmon garnished with more watercress and lemon quarters.

FISH AND MUSHROOM PIE

1 lb haddock (450 g)
½ pint milk (300 ml)
1 tablespoon fresh herbs
4 oz mushrooms, wiped and chopped (110 g)
1 oz butter (25 g)
½ teaspoon freshly grated nutmeg
1 tablespoon plain flour
salt and freshly ground black pepper
12 oz ready made puff pastry (350 g)

Poach the haddock for 15 minutes with the herbs, milk and a little seasoning. Strain and reserve the milk. Flake the fish, discarding skin and bones. Melt half the butter and sweat the mushrooms. Melt the rest of the butter in another pan, add the flour and make a roux, then stir in the milk. Add the nutmeg and some salt and pepper, and cook gently for two minutes. Mix the fish, sauce and mushrooms together. Roll out the pastry, divide in two, and place one half on a dampened baking sheet. Pile the filling on top, wet the edges and put the other half of pastry on top. Press the edges together and flute. Brush with milk or beaten egg. Bake at Gas 7, 425 deg F, 220 deg C, for 30–40 minutes until risen and golden brown, reducing the heat a little after the first 15 minutes.

FISH CAKES

My children love these fish cakes, and I like them because I know exactly what has gone into them, which is more than I can say for commercial fish cakes. Do not be tempted to alter the proportions of fish and mashed potatoes in favour of fish or they will fall to bits.

8 oz white fish, cooked and flaked (250 g)
12 oz potatoes, cooked and mashed (350 g)
salt and freshly ground black pepper
1 tablespoon fresh parsley, finely chopped
¼ teaspoon freshly grated nutmeg
1 small egg, beaten
3 oz dry brown breadcrumbs (75 g)
oil for frying

Combine the cooked fish and potatoes with the seasoning, parsley and nutmeg. Form into eight even-sized rounds, dip them in egg, then into the breadcrumbs, and fry in hot oil for four or five minutes on each side. You can prepare these fishcakes in advance and keep them in the fridge until needed; they also freeze well.

FISH CHOWDER

A chowder is a cross between a soup and a stew. We eat this one from large bowls with plenty of crusty bread to mop up the juices.

1 lb white fish (450 g)
8 oz potatoes, peeled or scraped and roughly grated (225 g)
1 large onion, peeled and chopped
1 sprig thyme
1 blade mace
pared zest of a lemon
salt and freshly ground black pepper
2 tablespoons sunflower oil
½ a bunch of watercress, washed
2 tomatoes, skinned and quartered

Make a fish stock by simmering 1 pint (600 ml) water, the lemon zest, herbs, salt and pepper, and the skin and bones of the fish for about 20 minutes. Meanwhile, trim the fish into large chunks. Heat the oil in a heavy-based pan, then soften the onion. Add the grated potato, stirring well to coat in oil. Then add the fish and the strained stock, bring to the boil, then turn down the heat and simmer uncovered for 30 minutes. Stir in the tomatoes and watercress, heat through, and serve at once.

HADDOCK WITH MUSHROOMS

2 large haddock fillets
a little butter
4 oz mushrooms, wiped and sliced (110 g)
1 small onion, peeled and finely chopped
1 clove garlic, crushed
¼ pint dry cider (150 ml)
1 sprig rosemary
2 oz fresh brown breadcrumbs (55 g)
salt and freshly ground black pepper

Lay the haddock flat in a large buttered baking dish. Sprinkle the onion, mushrooms and garlic over the fish, and season with salt and plenty of pepper. Tuck in the rosemary, pour in the cider, sprinkle the breadcrumbs over the top, and cover with foil or a lid. Bake in the oven at Gas 6, 400 deg F, 200 deg C for 30 minutes, uncovering during the last five minutes. Serve with a crisp green salad.
Serves 2.

HAKE AND POTATO BAKE

1 lb potatoes, scrubbed or peeled and sliced thinly (450 g)
2 oz butter (55 g)
1 lb skinned hake fillets, cut into 1 inch (2.5 cm) pieces (450 g)
4 oz mushrooms, wiped and sliced (110 g)
2 tablespoons milk
1 tablespoon fresh parsley, finely chopped
salt and freshly ground black pepper

Boil the sliced potatoes in salted boiling water for three or four minutes. Drain. Grease an ovenproof dish with half the butter, then layer the potatoes, fish and mushrooms in the dish, sprinkling in salt, pepper and parsley as you go. Finish with a layer of potatoes. Drizzle in the milk, dot the top with the remaining butter and bake uncovered for 20–25 minutes at Gas 6, 400 deg F, 200 deg C. Test with a sharp knife to check that fish and potatoes are cooked; if it slides in easily, the dish is ready.
Serves 3–4.

HAKE IN WHITE WINE

1 lb small new potatoes (450 g)
8 oz mushrooms, wiped (225 g)
1 lb tomatoes, skinned (450 g)
1 small onion, peeled
1 bulb fennel, trimmed
4 large hake cutlets
$\frac{1}{4}$ pint dry white wine (150 ml)
1 tablespoon olive oil
salt and freshly ground black pepper

to garnish:
lemon slices and fennel fronds

Scrub or peel and slice the potatoes, then boil in salted water for five minutes. Drain and place in an ovenproof dish. Slice the mushrooms, tomatoes, onion and fennel, and place on top of the potatoes. Arrange the fish on top, and pour over the wine and olive oil. Add a little salt and plenty of pepper. Cover with a lid or foil, and bake for 30–40 minutes at Gas 5, 375 deg F, 190 deg C. The fish will be opaque and will flake easily with a fork when cooked.

ITALIAN SEAFOOD RISOTTO

12 oz risotto rice (350 g)
14 oz mussels, scrubbed and beards removed (400 g)
7 fl oz dry white wine (200 ml)
approx 1 pint fish stock (600 ml)
2 oz butter (55 g)
1 small onion, peeled and finely chopped
4 oz shelled prawns (110 g)
4 scallops, sliced

to serve:
extra butter

Partly cook the rice in plenty of salted water for six minutes, then drain. Place the mussels and wine in a pan and cook over a high heat for three or four minutes until the mussels open. Remove the mussels from their shells, discarding any that have not opened. Strain the cooking liquor, then reduce it by half, and make it up to $1\frac{1}{2}$ pints (900 ml) with fish stock. Finish cooking the rice in this liquid. In another pan, melt the butter and soften the onion, then add the mussels, prawns and scallops and cook gently for two or three minutes. Keep warm. Drain the rice when cooked and stir in the onions, mussels, prawns and scallops. Season if necessary, and serve very hot dotted with extra butter.

MACKEREL IN CIDER

2 medium sized mackerel, cleaned
1 red onion, peeled and sliced thinly
$\frac{1}{2}$ pint cider (300 ml)
2 tablespoons fresh parsley, chopped
1 or 2 teaspoons cornflour

Put the onions in the base of a baking dish and arrange the mackerel side by side on top. Place a tablespoon of parsley in each body cavity. Pour the cider over the fish and cover with a lid or foil. Bake at Gas 4, 350 deg F, 180 deg C for 30–40 minutes or until the mackerel are cooked; when you can easily slide a knife into the thickest part of the flesh, they are ready. Remove mackerel and onions to a hot serving plate, and keep warm. Pour the cooking liquor into a pan, take off a couple of tablespoonfuls and mix to a paste with the cornflour, return to the pan, and bring to the boil, stirring well. Pour over the fish. Serve very hot with boiled new potatoes and a green vegetable.
Serves 2.

MACKEREL WITH HERBS

Mackerel is an excellent fish if fresh, revolting if anything less. It is at its best from August to May, and you should look for fish with clear blue, black and silver markings and bright eyes.

> *for each person, you need:*
> *1 smallish mackerel, gutted*
> *a squeeze of lemon juice*
> *a little olive oil*
> *a few sprigs and leaves of fresh herbs, tied into a bunch*

Take the heads off the fish and bone them. (You can ask your fishmonger to do this, but it's not a difficult job with a sharp knife and a pair of tweezers.) Squeeze a little lemon juice into the body cavity of each fish, then place a bunch of herbs inside. Fasten the opening carefully with a cocktail stick. Pat the skin dry, then brush well with olive oil and grill for five minutes on each side, remembering to brush the grill bars with olive oil to prevent sticking. Serve with potatoes or rice and salad.

PRAWN, SPINACH AND MUSHROOM PIE

1 lb pack frozen filo pastry (450 g)
1 lb fresh spinach (450 g)
6 oz low fat cream cheese (75 g)
1 teaspoon freshly grated nutmeg
12 oz mushrooms, wiped and sliced (350 g)
4 oz unsalted butter (110 g)
1 teaspoon fresh thyme leaves
$\frac{1}{4}$ pint double cream (150 ml)
8 oz shelled prawns (225 g)
salt and freshly ground black pepper
1 tablespoon sesame seeds

Defrost the filo pastry while you prepare the filling. Wash the spinach and cook it in just the water adhering to its leaves; when tender, drain thoroughly, chop well, then mash in the cream cheese, the grated nutmeg, plenty of pepper and a little salt.

While the spinach is cooking, prepare the mushrooms; sweat them gently in half the butter until they are just cooked. Take off the heat and drain, reserving the buttery juices. Mix the mushrooms with the thyme, cream, prawns and some salt and pepper. Melt the rest of the butter with the saved juices from the mushrooms, and use some of it to brush a large shallow ovenproof dish.
Make layers of half the filo pastry leaves, bringing them up and slightly over the edges of the dish, and brushing each layer with melted butter. Now spoon the spinach mixture into the base of the pie, and cover with the mushroom and prawn mixture. Use the rest of the filo leaves to cover the filling, brushing with melted butter as before. When you have finished, trim the edges off with a sharp knife, fan them out a bit, and brush with melted butter. Make a criss-cross pattern on top of the pie with a sharp knife, cutting quite deeply into the pastry.

Use the rest of the melted butter to brush the top, then sprinkle with sesame seeds and bake for 40–50 minutes at Gas 6, 400 deg C, 200 deg C, until the pie is cooked through. If the top or the edges of the pie look like over-browning after 25 minutes, cover with greased foil. Serve hot.
Serves 6–8.

SALMON EN CROUTE

Frozen puff pastry is a boon to the busy cook, not only because she can make wonderful creations without taking hours over the pastry, but also because it can be used to wrap a relatively expensive filling and thus make it go further.

2 sheets ready-rolled puff pastry, measuring about 8 × 8 inches (20 × 20 cm)
1½ lb piece fresh salmon (700 g)
6 spring onions
2 oz mushrooms, wiped (55 g)
a few parsley stalks
6 peppercorns
1 tablespoon dry white wine
¼ pint double cream (150 ml)
milk or beaten egg for brushing

Ask your fishmonger to skin and bone the fish for you; he may divide it into two fillets or just leave you with one piece. Ask for the skin and bones, as you will need them for stock.

Chop the whites of the spring onions, heat the butter in a skillet or small frying pan, and soften. Chop the mushrooms finely and add to the pan with some freshly ground black pepper.

Place the fish on one of the pieces of pastry. When the mushrooms and onions are soft, remove from the heat and use half to stuff the salmon. Lay the other piece of pastry on top, and press down the sides, brushing them first with water. Trim, making an oval fish shape and using the trimmings for fins and an eye. Mark scales into the pastry with a sharp knife. Brush with milk or beaten egg, and bake on a tray lined with baking parchment at Gas 6, 400 deg F, 200 deg C for 35–40 minutes, covering with more baking parchment or greased foil if the pastry begins to brown too quickly.

Meanwhile, simmer the fish skin and bones with the parsley and peppercorns for about 15 minutes. Strain. Return the stock to the pan and reduce to about ¼ pint (150 ml). Put the mushrooms and onions back on the heat, add the stock and wine, if using, and reduce by half. Keep warm, then when ready to serve, place back on the heat, add the cream and heat through. Serve with the salmon, together with boiled potatoes and fresh seasonal vegetables.
Serves 4–6.

SEA BREAM MEUNIERE

4 good thick fillets sea bream
4 tablespoons plain flour
salt and freshly ground black pepper
4 oz butter (110 g)
1 tablespoon fresh parsley, chopped
juice of a lemon

Season the flour with salt and pepper, then use it to coat the fish. Heat half the butter in one large or two medium-sized frying pans and fry the fish for about ten minutes, until browned, turning once. Remove the fillets from the pan, place them on four plates and sprinkle each with parsley and lemon juice. Keep warm. Add the remaining butter to the frying pan, and melt. When golden and bubbling, pour over the fish and serve at once.

SEA BREAM WITH APPLE

2 fillets of sea bream
3 rashers streaky bacon, finely chopped
1 medium onion, peeled and finely chopped
1 clove garlic, crushed
1 tablespoon brandy
$\frac{1}{4}$ pint fish stock (150 ml)
juice of $\frac{1}{2}$ an orange
1 tablespoon fresh parsley, finely chopped
1 large eating apple, peeled, cored and sliced
$\frac{1}{2}$ oz butter (15 g)

Using a sharp knife, scrape the scales off the fish skin if your fishmonger has not already done so. Gently heat the streaky bacon in a medium-sized frying pan until the fat runs, then add the onion and garlic and cook gently. There should be enough fat in the bacon to cook the onion, but if there is not, add a very little vegetable oil. Lightly butter a baking dish, then place the onion, garlic, bacon and parsley in the bottom. Arrange the fish fillets on top. Pour the stock, brandy, and orange juice into the frying pan and bring to the boil, scraping up any bits left on the bottom of the pan. Pour over the fish. Arrange the slices of apple down the centre of the dish, cover with foil greased with the rest of the butter, and bake for 20 - 25 minutes at Gas 6, 400 deg F, 200 deg C until the flesh is white and tender. Serve at once with sauté potatoes and French beans. For a special occasion, the dish looks good garnished with parsley and very thinly pared strips of orange peel.
Serves 2.

SEAFOOD THERMIDOR

I am told that this is an unfashionable dish nowadays, presumably because it is rather rich in calories. However, it is undoubtedly a wonderful dish and deserves to be made from time to time in defiance of those foodies who say we should disdain flour-based sauces.

> 1 lemon sole, skinned and in two fillets, weighing about 10 oz (275 g)
> 6 oz monkfish or other firm white fish (175 g)
> 2 scallops
> 4 oz fat prawns (110 g)
> juice and grated zest of $\frac{1}{2}$ a lemon
> 8 fresh parsley stalks
> $\frac{1}{4}$ pint dry white wine (150 ml)
> $\frac{1}{4}$ pint water (150 ml)
> 3 oz butter (75 g)
> $1\frac{1}{2}$ oz plain flour (40 g)
> 4 oz mushrooms, wiped and sliced (110 g)
> $\frac{1}{2}$ teaspoon English mustard powder
> $\frac{1}{4}$ teaspoon cayenne pepper
> $\frac{1}{4}$ pint double cream (150 ml)
> 2 oz Cheddar cheese, grated (55 g)
> 1 oz fresh brown breadcrumbs (25 g)
> salt and freshly ground black pepper
> 1 teaspoon paprika

Ask your fishmonger to prepare the lemon sole for you; keep the skin and bones. Place these and any other fish trimmings in a saucepan with the lemon juice and zest, parsley stalks, wine and water. Bring to the boil, skim, cover, and simmer for ten minutes.

Meanwhile, chop the fish into bite-sized pieces and slice the scallops. Place fish and scallops in a lightly buttered gratin or shallow ovenproof dish. In another saucepan, melt 2 oz (55 g) of the butter, stir in the flour, and cook gently for one minute. Strain the stock, discard the bones, etc, and slowly add the stock to the butter and flour roux, stirring well. Add the sliced mushrooms, mustard powder and cayenne pepper and cook very gently.

Melt the remaining 1 oz (25 g) butter, brush over the fish in the gratin dish, sprinkle on a little salt, place under a hot grill and cook for about ten minutes. The fish will go white and opaque when it is cooked—remove from the heat at once. Sprinkle the prawns on top. Stir the double cream into the sauce, season with salt and pepper, and pour over the fish. Sprinkle the breadcrumbs and cheese on top, and sprinkle on a little paprika and black pepper. Place under the grill again for five minutes. Serve at once, with boiled new potatoes and green beans or a robust salad.

SKATE BAKED WITH GREEN OLIVES

2 wings of skate
juice of ½ a large lemon
1 oz butter (25 g)
2 teaspoons white wine vinegar
12 green olives, stoned and halved
salt and freshly ground black pepper

to garnish:
2 tablespoons fresh parsley, finely chopped

Grease a large baking dish with half the butter, then place the fish side by side in it. Sprinkle over the lemon juice and vinegar, add the halved olives, and dot with the rest of the butter. Season with a little salt and pepper. Cover with a lid or buttered foil, and bake in the oven at Gas 5, 375 deg F, 190 deg C, for 20–30 minutes. The exact cooking time will depend on the size of the fish; it is ready when the flesh is quite white and opaque. Before serving, scrape the thin membrane off the top side of the fish with a spoon or small knife. Serve with the olives and the cooking liquor poured over, and sprinkled liberally with parsley.
Serves 2.

SKATE WITH BLACK BUTTER

4 skate wings
2 tablespoons white wine vinegar
1 bay leaf
4 parsley stalks
3 oz butter (75 g)
1 tablespoon capers
2 teaspoons lemon juice
salt and freshly ground black pepper

Place the skate wings side by side in a large frying pan, add the vinegar and herbs, and pour on enough water just to cover the fish. Bring to the boil, then turn down the heat, cover and simmer gently for 10–15 minutes. Meanwhile, gently melt the butter in a small pan, then tip the golden liquid into another pan, leaving behind the white sediment, which you should discard. Heat until it begins to go brown, then stir in the capers, a little salt and pepper, and the lemon juice. Remove from the heat. Drain the cooked fish, pour the sauce over, and serve with plain boiled fluffy white rice.

SOMERSET FISH

1½ lb thick white fish fillets (700 g)
8 rashers streaky bacon, chopped small
1 large dessert apple, peeled, cored and sliced
¼ pint dry cider (150 ml)
6 fresh sage leaves, chopped
1 tablespoon cornflour

Place the fish in a shallow casserole dish, and scatter the bacon over the top. Arrange the apple slices in a pretty pattern over the top, tuck in the sage leaves, and pour the cider over. Sprinkle with a very little salt and pepper. Bake at Gas 7, 425 deg F, 220 deg C for 20–25 minutes, or until the fish feels tender. Drain off the juices into a small saucepan and keep the fish warm in the oven. Mix the cornflour with a little cooking juice, return to the pan, then bring to the boil, stirring all the time. Check the seasoning, then pour over the fish. Remove the sage leaves and serve hot.

SPANISH PAELLA
Shellfish, chicken and rice

12 chicken thighs or drumsticks
3–4 tablespoons olive oil
a good pinch of saffron strands
1 pint chicken stock (600 ml)
1 large onion, peeled and chopped
1 clove garlic, crushed
12 oz risotto rice (350 g)
14 oz tin tomatoes (400 g)
1 red pepper, deseeded and chopped
1 pint mussels, in shells
10 prawns, in shells
12 black olives
1 lemon

Heat the oil in a very large frying pan or a flameproof casserole, and fry the chicken pieces until brown all over. Continue cooking more gently for 10–15 minutes. Meanwhile, infuse the saffron strands in the chicken stock, which will go bright yellow. Add the onion to the chicken in the pan and allow it to soften for a few minutes, then add the garlic, rice, and chicken stock. Cover, and cook for 15 minutes. Drain the tomatoes, chop them roughly, and add to the pan with the chopped red pepper. Place the mussels on top, cover, and continue cooking very gently. After 20 minutes, the mussels should have opened; discard any that have not. Now tuck the prawns down into the rice and cook for another five minutes. Garnish with black olives, and serve straight from the pan, along with slices of lemon, finger bowls, and plates for the shellfish debris.
Serves 6.

SPICY FISH

Fish in a curried sauce sounds rather unpleasant, but actually it works very well. Gentle cooking is the secret to this recipe.

   1 lb cod, haddock or any fresh white fish, cut into bite-sized pieces (450 g)
   1 tablespoon oil
   1 onion, peeled and chopped
   1 clove garlic, crushed
   1 inch piece root ginger, peeled and crushed (2.5 cm)
   1 teaspoon turmeric
   2 teaspoons curry powder
   8 oz thick plain yogurt (225 g)
   $\frac{1}{2}$ teaspoon salt

Heat the oil in a large frying pan and gently soften the onion for a few minutes. Stir in the garlic and ginger, cook for a few more minutes, then add the turmeric and curry powder and mix in well. Add the yogurt and cook gently for five minutes, stirring now and then. Now add the fish and salt and cook gently for five to ten minutes, until the fish flakes easily and is cooked through. Serve with rice.
Serves 2.

TROUT WITH HERBS AND LEMON

   2 fresh trout, cleaned and weighing about 8 oz (225 g) each
   2 tablespoons plain flour
   salt and freshly ground black pepper
   3 oz unsalted butter (75 g)
   juice and grated zest of $\frac{1}{2}$ a lemon
   1 teaspoon each thyme and tarragon leaves
   2 teaspoons fresh parsley, finely chopped

Coat the fish with the seasoned flour. Gently melt 2 oz (55 g) of butter in a large frying pan, then fry the fish for six or seven minutes on each side. Do not overcook; test the tenderness of the flesh with a sharp knife. Place on absorbent kitchen paper in a dish and keep warm. Wipe out the frying pan with more kitchen paper, and melt the rest of the butter. Add the lemon juice and zest, herbs, a pinch of salt and a good twist of the pepper mill. Place the fish on warmed plates, pour the pan juices over, and serve at once. This is good with sauté or Lyonnaise potatoes and green beans.
Serves 2.

TUNA BAKED IN RED WINE AND HERBS

Fresh tuna is not always easy to obtain, but it's worth tracking down. The skin is dark blue on top, silvery on the sides and underneath. The flesh is a deep reddish-pink and very heavy, almost like meat. It is best served with the kind of sauce you would offer with meat; red wine makes an excellent cooking medium.

2 fresh tuna steaks
1 red onion, skinned and thinly sliced
1 clove garlic, crushed
a sprig of thyme, a crushed bay leaf, 6 parsley stalks
1 tablespoon lemon juice
1 tablespoon good olive oil
$\frac{1}{4}$ pint red wine (150 ml)
salt and freshly ground black pepper

to garnish:
1 tablespoon fresh parsley, chopped

Lay the tuna steaks in a shallow non-metal ovenproof dish with the sliced onions, garlic and herbs. Sprinkle over the lemon juice, olive oil, a little salt and lots of freshly ground black pepper, and allow to marinate at room temperature for an hour. Pour in the wine, cover with a lid or greased foil, and bake for 20–30 minutes at Gas 6, 400 deg F, 200 deg C; push a sharp knife into the thickest part of the fish, and if it flakes easily, it is cooked. Sprinkle on the parsley, and serve hot, with rice or lots of French bread and a crunchy green salad made with strongly flavoured leaves and a few black olives if you like them.
Serves 2.

POULTRY & GAME

Chicken · Pheasant · Rabbit · Duck · Turkey

POULTRY AND GAME

Many of the recipes in this section are for chicken, because it is so popular. Most of them can also be used for turkey.

If you have ever seen hens at large, you will know how they enjoy roaming around, pecking, arguing among themselves and generally setting the world to rights. They are infuriating, wilful, cheeky birds, but having seen how they behave when left more or less to themselves, I could never again buy a bird that had been kept in a cage all its life.

So I always buy free range chickens and turkeys. Although they are more expensive, they still make a reasonably economical meal, and undoubtedly have a better flavour and texture. For a change, it's well worth experimenting with duck and pheasant; and I thoroughly recommend rabbit to anyone who hasn't tried it; it's full of flavour and as tender as chicken. Again, it's best to buy wild rabbit rather than farmed.

Catalan chicken
Chicken and avocado salad
Chicken and broccoli au gratin
Chicken and pineapple salad
Chicken cacciatore (Italian chicken casserole)
Chicken chasseur
Chicken in cider
Chicken risotto with prawns
Chicken with lime and ginger
Chicken with prunes and bacon
Chicken with tarragon and lemon
Coronation turkey salad
Coq au vin
Curried turkey
Duck with mango sauce

Pheasant casserole
Poule au pot (French country casserole with vegetables)
Rabbit casserole
Rabbit Provençale
Roast pheasant with game chips
Spicy chicken with yogurt
Stir fried turkey
Stuffed chicken breasts with fresh tomato sauce
Stuffed turkey breasts
Summer chicken casserole
Tipsy turkey
Turkey tikka
Turkey with nuts and honey

CATALAN CHICKEN

4 large or 8 small chicken pieces
4 tablespoons olive oil
1 onion, peeled and finely chopped
1 or 2 cloves garlic, crushed
1 large red pepper, deseeded and sliced
4 tablespoons sweet sherry
4 large tomatoes, skinned and chopped
salt and freshly ground black pepper
8 black olives, stoned and halved

Heat the oil and fry the chicken pieces until golden brown. Remove them and keep warm while you soften the onion, garlic and red pepper for about five minutes in the same pan, stirring now and then. Replace the chicken pieces, season, and add the sherry. Cook for a few minutes over a gentle heat, then add the chopped tomatoes. Cover and cook gently for 25–30 minutes. Five minutes before the chicken is cooked through, add the black olives. Serve hot with rice.

CHICKEN AND BROCCOLI AU GRATIN

12 oz cold cooked chicken in large chunks (350 g)
8 oz broccoli spears (225 g)
2 oz butter (55 g)
1½ oz flour (40 g)
1 pint milk (600 ml)
2 oz farmhouse Cheddar, grated (55 g)
¼ teaspoon nutmeg, freshly grated
salt and freshly ground black pepper

Bring a large saucepan of lightly salted water to the boil and plunge in the broccoli. Cook for five minutes until just tender. Drain. Make the white sauce while the broccoli is cooking by melting the butter, then stirring in the flour to make a roux. Add the milk little by little, stirring well to get rid of all the lumps. Add the grated cheese, nutmeg and some salt and pepper, and cook very gently for five minutes, stirring now and then. Arrange the broccoli and chicken in a shallow baking dish, pour the sauce over the top and bake at Gas 5, 375 deg F, 190 deg C for 25–30 minutes. Serve with crusty bread.
Serves 2–3.

CHICKEN CACCIATORE
Italian style chicken with tomatoes

8 small chicken pieces
1 lemon, cut into wedges
2 oz plain flour (55 g)
2 tablespoons olive oil
2 tablespoons brandy
2 oz butter (55 g)
14 oz tin Italian tomatoes, chopped roughly (400 g)
¼ pint red wine (150 ml)
1 clove garlic, crushed
1 tablespoon fresh basil, chopped, or 1 teaspoon dried basil
salt and freshly ground black pepper
12 shallots, peeled
2 green peppers, deseeded and cut into thin strips
8 oz button mushrooms, wiped (225 g)

to garnish:
fresh parsley or basil

Start by rubbing the chicken pieces with the lemon wedges, then coat them in plain flour. Heat the oil in a large flameproof casserole, add the chicken pieces, and fry on all sides until golden brown. Add the brandy, half the butter, the tomatoes and their juice, the wine, garlic, dried basil and some salt and freshly ground black pepper. (If you are using fresh basil, add it 20 minutes before the end of the cooking time.) Bring to the boil, reduce the heat, cover and simmer for 15 minutes. Add the shallots and peppers, cover and simmer for another 15–25 minutes, until the vegetables and chicken are tender. Ten minutes before serving, melt the remaining butter and gently cook the mushrooms for about five minutes. Drain, and add to the chicken. If the sauce looks a bit thin, pour most of it off into a small pan and boil hard to reduce and thicken it, then pour over the chicken. Sprinkle chopped parsley or basil leaves on the chicken and serve.

CHICKEN CHASSEUR

4 large or 8 small chicken pieces
2 tablespoons olive oil
1 oz butter (25 g)
4 oz mushrooms, wiped and sliced (110 g)
2–3 shallots, peeled and quartered
6 tablespoons dry white wine
1 tablespoon tomato purée
1 tablespoon brandy
1 tablespoon each fresh tarragon and parsley, finely chopped
salt and freshly ground black pepper

Heat the oil and butter together in a large frying pan and sauté the chicken pieces so that they are golden brown on all sides and cooked through. Transfer them to a warmed plate and keep warm in the oven while you prepare the sauce. Sauté the mushrooms in the pan juices for five minutes or until soft, then add the shallots and allow them to soften. Now add the white wine and tomato purée, turn up the heat and reduce by half. Add the brandy, tarragon, salt and pepper to taste, bring to the boil, then pour over the chicken. Sprinkle with the parsley and serve at once.

CHICKEN IN CIDER

4 large chicken breasts
1½ oz plain flour (40 g)
salt and freshly ground black pepper
1 oz butter (25 g)
1 clove garlic, crushed
1 onion, peeled and sliced
½ pint dry or medium cider (300 ml)
4 oz mushrooms, wiped and sliced (110 g)
16 black olives
4 tablespoons double cream (optional)

to garnish:
1 tablespoon parsley, chopped

Mix the flour with some salt and pepper and coat the chicken pieces. Melt the butter in a flameproof casserole, then brown the chicken pieces on all sides. Remove and keep warm, and soften the onion and garlic in the same pan. Replace the chicken, add the cider, cover, and transfer to the oven. Bake for 30 minutes at Gas 4, 350 deg F, 180 deg C. Add the mushrooms and olives, and cook for another 15 minutes or until the chicken is tender. Stir in the cream, if using, just before serving.

CHICKEN RISOTTO WITH PRAWNS

1 or 2 chicken breasts, weighing about 8 oz (225 g)
1 onion, peeled and finely chopped
1 clove garlic, crushed
2 pints chicken stock (1.25 litres)
8 oz risotto rice (225 g)
½ teaspoon powdered saffron (optional)
salt and freshly ground black pepper
4 oz frozen peas (110 g)
4 oz peeled prawns (110 g)

to garnish:
1 tablespoon fresh parsley, chopped, and 6 whole prawns

Cut the chicken into neat, bite sized pieces. Place all the ingredients except the peas, prawns and garnish in a large saucepan. Bring to the boil, then turn down the heat and simmer, uncovered, for 35 minutes. By this time the chicken should be tender and the rice just about cooked. Stir in the peas and prawns and turn up the heat. Cook for another five minutes or so, stirring from time to time, until the peas are tender and all the liquid has been absorbed. Check the seasoning then turn the risotto out on to a warm plate, sprinkle with the chopped parsley, and garnish with the whole prawns.

CHICKEN WITH LIME AND GINGER

4 chicken breasts, skinned
juice and grated zest of a lime
small piece of root ginger, peeled and grated
¼ pint white wine or dry cider (150 ml)
salt and freshly ground black pepper
1 oz butter (25 g)

to garnish:
2 slices of fresh lime

Marinate the chicken in the wine, ginger, lime zest and juice for a couple of hours before cooking. When ready to cook, melt the butter in a frying pan, pat the chicken breasts dry and fry them for five minutes or so, turning them now and then. Now pour the marinade ingredients over the chicken, season, and cook gently for another 10–15 minutes, until the chicken is tender and the sauce has thickened up. Garnish with a twist of lime and serve with a green salad and rice.
Serves 2.

CHICKEN WITH PRUNES AND BACON

4 large or 8 small chicken portions
4 oz large, stoned prunes (110 g)
1 oz butter (25 g)
8 oz smoked streaky bacon, chopped (225 g)
1 onion, peeled and chopped
1 large carrot, scrubbed and chopped
2 sticks celery, scrubbed and chopped
1½ oz plain flour (40 g)
¼ pint red wine (150 ml)
¾ pint chicken stock (450 ml)
finely grated rind of an orange
salt and freshly ground black pepper

Soak the prunes in water overnight. Drain. Melt the butter in a large frying pan, and then add the chopped streaky bacon. When the fat runs, add the chicken and brown it on all sides. Remove it from the pan and keep warm in an ovenproof casserole. Add the onion, carrot and celery to the pan and fry for five minutes, stirring frequently. Stir in the flour, then add the remaining ingredients and bring to the boil. Turn down the heat and simmer for a few minutes until the sauce thickens. Pour over the chicken, cover the casserole tightly, and cook at Gas 4, 350 deg F, 180 deg C for 1½ hours or until the chicken is tender.

CHICKEN WITH TARRAGON AND LEMON

4 large or 8 small chicken pieces
2 oz butter (55 g)
2 tablespoons sunflower oil
1 onion, peeled and finely chopped
juice and grated zest of 2 lemons
1 tablespoon plain flour
½ pint chicken stock (300 ml)
¼ pint dry white wine (150 ml)
1 tablespoon fresh tarragon leaves
2 tablespoons double cream
salt and freshly ground black pepper

Pat the chicken pieces dry, prick with a fork, and sprinkle with a little of the lemon juice and some salt and pepper. Heat the oil and butter together in a large frying pan or flameproof casserole, and brown the chicken pieces. Remove and keep warm, then place the onion in the casserole and soften. Stir in the flour and cook for one minute. Add the wine, chicken stock, lemon juice and zest, and bring to the boil. Turn down the heat and add the tarragon, chicken pieces, and some more salt and pepper if needed. Cover tightly and simmer for 30 minutes or until the chicken is cooked. Remove the chicken and keep it warm. Reduce the cooking juices by half, stir in the cream and heat through gently, then pour over the chicken. Serve with rice.

CORONATION TURKEY SALAD

2 lb cold cooked turkey, diced (1 kg)
1 tablespoon oil
1 small onion, peeled and diced
1 tablespoon curry paste
1 teaspoon tomato purée
juice of ½ a lemon
4 or 5 no-need-to-soak apricots, chopped small
¼ pint bought mayonnaise (150 ml)
1 tablespoon double cream
2 oz flaked almonds (55 g)
salt and freshly ground black pepper

to serve:
lettuce leaves and sprigs of watercress

Heat the oil in a small saucepan and sauté the onion until soft, then add the curry paste, tomato purée and lemon juice. Cook gently for about five minutes, then take off the heat and allow to cool. When cool, mix with the apricots, mayonnaise, cream and flaked almonds. Season with salt and freshly ground black pepper, and add more lemon juice if you think it needs it. Fold in the cooked, chopped turkey, and serve on a bed of lettuce, garnished with sprigs of watercress.

COQ AU VIN

A cock bird, with its pronounced flavour and firm texture, really does work well with the strong flavours of this classic dish. However, a chicken will do if you can't get a cock bird.

1 oven-ready cock bird (or large chicken)
2 tablespoons olive oil
8 oz streaky bacon, chopped (225 g)
1 large onion, peeled and chopped
1 clove garlic, crushed
1 green pepper, deseeded and chopped
1 pint red wine (600 ml)

2 sprigs thyme
1 bay leaf, crushed
salt and freshly ground black pepper
4 oz mushrooms, wiped and sliced (110 g)

to garnish:
fresh parsley

Joint the bird. Heat the oil in a large flameproof casserole, then fry the pieces a few at a time until browned on all sides. Remove and keep warm. Add the onions, garlic and bacon to the casserole and fry for five minutes, stirring frequently, then replace the cock or chicken pieces, and add the green pepper, wine, herbs and some seasoning. Cover and simmer gently for two or three hours, topping up with more wine, water, or chicken stock if needed. Add the mushrooms about 15 minutes before the end of the cooking time. Garnish with fresh parsley, and serve with sauté potatoes and a green salad.
Serves 6.

CURRIED TURKEY

$1\frac{1}{2}$ lb cooked turkey meat (700 g)
2 tablespoons sunflower oil
1 clove garlic, crushed
1 large onion, peeled and chopped
1 green pepper, deseeded and chopped
1 stick celery, scrubbed and chopped
2 tablespoons plain flour
2 teaspoons hot curry powder
1 teaspoon each ground ginger and turmeric
1 pint turkey or chicken stock (600 ml)
2 oz sultanas (55 g)
1 tablespoon lemon juice

Heat the oil in a heavy-based saucepan and soften the onion and garlic. Add the pepper and celery and continue cooking for another five minutes or so, until soft. Add the flour, spices and curry powder and stir well. When all the juices have been absorbed, add the chicken stock little by little, stirring well. Cover and simmer for 15 minutes. Meanwhile, chop the turkey meat into neat pieces. Add the meat and sultanas to the pan and heat through. Stir in the lemon juice and serve with pilau rice.

DUCK WITH MANGO SAUCE

4 fresh duck portions
1 tablespoon salt
1 ripe mango
2 teaspoons brown sugar
1 tablespoon white wine vinegar

to garnish:
sprigs of watercress

Prick the skin of the duck with a sharp knife, then rub a little salt all over the skin. Place on a rack over a roasting dish, and bake in the oven for 60–75 minutes at Gas 6, 400 deg F, 200 deg C, basting occasionally. To see if the duck is ready, prick the thickest part with a sharp knife and if the juices run clear, it is cooked. Cut the mango into quarters and pull each quarter away from the stone in the centre. Skin each quarter; discard skin and stone. Mash the flesh from two quarters and slice the remaining quarters thinly. In a small pan, melt the sugar in the vinegar over a gentle heat, and cook for a couple of minutes. Add the pulped mango flesh and cook gently for 5 minutes to make a thick, orange sauce. Serve with the duck, garnished with watercress and the remaining mango slices.

PHEASANT CASSEROLE

1 brace oven-ready pheasants
1 oz flour (25 g)
1 oz lard (25 g)
2 rashers streaky bacon, chopped
1 onion, peeled and chopped
1 stick celery, scrubbed and chopped
1 tablespoon fresh parsley, chopped
1 sprig thyme and 1 bay leaf
1 pint chicken stock (600 ml)
$\frac{1}{4}$ pint dry red wine (150 ml)
2 oz mushrooms, wiped and sliced (55 g)
salt and freshly ground black pepper

Cut the birds into joints and dip each into the flour, seasoned with some salt and pepper. Melt the fat in a heavy-based casserole and fry each joint for a few minutes. Remove and keep warm. Add the onion, bacon and celery to the casserole, fry for five minutes, then replace the pheasant. Add the herbs, stock and wine. Check the seasoning. Cover and cook for $2\frac{1}{2}$–3 hours at Gas 3, 325 deg F, 170 deg C, adding the mushrooms 15 minutes before the end of the cooking time.

POULE AU POT
Casserole of chicken with vegetables

1 fresh chicken weighing about 3½ lb (1.5 kg), plus giblets
2 tablespoons olive oil
8 oz smoked streaky bacon, chopped (225 g)
1 clove garlic, crushed
12 shallots, peeled
1 onion, peeled and halved
8 small potatoes, scrubbed or peeled
4 carrots, scrubbed and chopped
4 baby turnips, scrubbed and quartered
¼ pint dry white wine (150 ml)
1 bay leaf, 1 sprig thyme, 6 parsley stalks, 6 celery leaves, tied in a bunch
8 oz mushrooms, wiped and sliced (225 g)
salt and freshly ground black pepper

Place the chicken giblets in a small pan, and add ½ pint (300 ml) of water and some salt and pepper. Bring to the boil and simmer for half an hour. Drain, discarding the giblets, and reduce the liquid to ¼ pint (150 ml). Reserve.

Heat the oil in a large flameproof casserole, and fry the streaky bacon until the fat runs, then add the garlic and shallots. Turn up the heat, allow to brown, then remove from the pan and keep warm.

Place the onion halves in the cavity of the chicken, then place it in the casserole and brown it all over, with the heat quite high. Put the chicken on its back and surround it with the bacon, garlic, shallots, potatoes, carrots and turnips. Pour in the white wine and the stock from the giblets. Add the herbs, some salt and pepper, and cover the casserole and cook at Gas 4, 350 deg F, 180 deg C for 1½ hours, or until the chicken and vegetables are tender.

Uncover during the last half hour, add the mushrooms, and leave uncovered, protecting the chicken breast with foil to stop it burning. When ready, remove the chicken from the pot, drain well, and serve surrounded with the well-drained vegetables. Reduce the cooking juices by rapid boiling and serve separately.

RABBIT CASSEROLE

1 young fresh rabbit, jointed
2 tablespoons seasoned flour
1 oz butter (25 g)
1 tablespoon sunflower oil
1 onion, peeled and chopped
3 carrots, scrubbed and chopped
2 sticks celery, scrubbed and chopped
$\frac{1}{4}$ pint white wine (150 ml)
$\frac{1}{2}$ pint chicken stock (300 ml)
4 oz button mushrooms, wiped and sliced (110 g)
1 tablespoon fresh parsley, chopped
salt and freshly ground black pepper

Heat the oil and butter in a flameproof casserole. Dip the rabbit joints in the seasoned flour, then fry quickly on all sides. Remove the browned rabbit joints and keep warm. In the same casserole, soften the onion, adding a little more oil if needed. Stir in the carrots and celery and cook for another five minutes. Replace the rabbit, pour in the wine and enough stock to cover the meat, bring to the boil, season, cover, and place in the oven. Cook for 40 minutes at Gas 4, 350 deg F, 180 deg C. Add the mushrooms and parsley, and cook for another 10 minutes. Strain off the cooking juices into a small pan and reduce by rapid boiling over a high heat. Pour over the rabbit and vegetables and serve at once.

RABBIT PROVENCALE

8 rabbit pieces
2 tablespoons seasoned flour
2 oz butter (55 g)
8 shallots, peeled
2 carrots, scrubbed and sliced
2 tablespoons Dijon mustard
$\frac{1}{4}$ pint each dry white wine and chicken stock (150 ml each)
1 tablespoon each oregano and thyme leaves
1 sprig rosemary
salt and freshly ground black pepper
4 oz button mushrooms, wiped and sliced (110 g)

Trim the rabbit pieces and coat in seasoned flour. Heat the butter in a flameproof casserole and brown the rabbit. Remove and keep warm, then sauté the shallots and carrots for a few minutes, stirring now and then. Replace the rabbit, add the mustard, wine, stock, and add salt and pepper to taste. Bring to the boil, reduce the heat, cover and simmer for about 40 minutes, stirring now and then. After 30 minutes add the sliced mushrooms to the pan together with the herbs. Remove the rosemary before serving. Serve with rice and a green vegetable.

ROAST PHEASANT AND GAME CHIPS

a brace of young pheasants
12 rashers smoked streaky bacon
1 onion, peeled and halved
1 lb even-sized potatoes, scrubbed or peeled (450 g)
oil for deep frying

Make sure the birds are clean inside and dry outside. Tuck a halved onion into the body cavity of each bird and lay them on their sides, side by side, on a rack over a tin to catch the juices. Cover each bird with six rashers of bacon. Roast for 15 minutes at Gas 7, 425 deg F, 220 deg C, then turn them over, replacing the bacon on the new side, and roast for another 15 minutes. Now turn the birds on to their backs, removing the bacon, and turn down the heat to Gas 6, 400 deg F, 200 deg C, and cook for another 15-30 minutes. Keep the bacon warm to serve with the birds. The birds are cooked when their juices run clear and the legs wiggle easily; you may find that the smaller hen cooks before the cock. Give them ten minutes resting time in a warm place before carving. To make the game chips, slice the potatoes very, very thinly. Deep fry them in hot oil until golden, frying batches if necessary and keeping the chips warm on kitchen paper in a dish in the oven. Serve with bread sauce and a thin gravy made from the juices, skimmed of fat, caught in the tin during cooking.

SPICY CHICKEN WITH YOGURT

1 pint thick set Greek yogurt (600 ml)
8 chicken breasts, skinned
3 or 4 garlic cloves, crushed
1 teaspoon each ground coriander, cumin, ginger and paprika
$\frac{1}{4}$ teaspoon each chilli powder and English mustard powder
$\frac{1}{2}$ inch (1 cm) piece root ginger, peeled and chopped small
half a fresh pineapple, peeled and sliced

In a large bowl, mix half the yogurt with the garlic and spices. Cut each chicken breast into two or three long pieces with a sharp knife and place them in the yogurt. Stir around to get all the pieces well coated, then cover and refrigerate overnight. When ready to cook, remove the chicken breasts and grill them for about ten minutes, turning once. Serve hot or cold with the unspiced $\frac{1}{2}$ pint of yogurt (300 ml) and the sliced pineapple.
Serves 4-6 as a main course, 6 as a starter, 8 as part of a buffet meal.

STIR FRIED TURKEY

2 turkey breasts, skinned
2–3 tablespoons sunflower oil
½ red pepper, deseeded
½ green pepper, deseeded
4 button mushrooms, wiped
white of a leek
2 small carrots, scrubbed
4 tablespoons soy sauce
2 teaspoons dark brown sugar
1 teaspoon cornflour
salt and freshly ground black pepper

Cut all the vegetables into neat, very thin slices before starting to cook. Cut the turkey breasts into 2 inch (5 cm) strips. Cream together the soy sauce, sugar, cornflour and some salt and freshly ground black pepper. Now heat the oil in a wok or very large frying pan until smoking hot. Fry the turkey for five minutes, stirring all the time. Add the peppers, mushrooms, leek and carrots, and continue frying and stirring, for another four or five minutes. Pour in the sauce and heat through, still stirring. Check the seasoning and serve at once with noodles or plain boiled rice.
Serves 2–3.

STUFFED CHICKEN BREASTS WITH FRESH TOMATO SAUCE

4 large chicken breasts, skinned
6 oz fresh spinach (175 g)
4 oz ripe Stilton cheese (110 g)
3 spring onions, finely chopped
1 tablespoon fresh tarragon, chopped
salt and freshly ground black pepper

for the tomato sauce:
1 onion, peeled and chopped
1 clove garlic, crushed
14 oz tin tomatoes (400 g)
1 tablespoon tomato purée

Wash the spinach and remove the stalks, then place in a large pan, add a little water, cover and cook gently until the leaves are wilted. Drain well, rinse in cold water, and pat dry. Place the chicken breasts under a clean tea towel and bash with a meat hammer or rolling pan until they have doubled in size. Line each breast with a layer of spinach leaves. Mash the cheese, onion, and half the tarragon with some salt and pepper until spreadable, then spread over the spinach. Roll each breast up as neatly as you can. Wrap individually in well-greased foil or baking parchment and place in a baking dish. Bake for 25 minutes at Gas 4, 350 deg F, 180 deg C, or until the chicken is tender. Meanwhile, make the tomato sauce by placing the onion, garlic, tomatoes, tomato purée, some salt and pepper, and the rest of the tarragon in a large frying pan and simmering gently until thick but not browned. Serve the chicken with the sauce and some rice or pasta.

STUFFED TURKEY BREASTS

2 turkey breasts, skinned
1 tablespoon corn or sunflower oil
6 dried apricots
2 tablespoons fresh breadcrumbs
2 pork sausages, skinned
1 oz blanched almonds, finely chopped (25 g)
½ teaspoon ground mixed spice
salt and freshly ground black pepper

To make the stuffing, pour boiling water over the apricots and soak them for 30 minutes. Drain, chop finely, and mash together with the sausagemeat, breadcrumbs, chopped almonds, spice and seasoning. Heat the oil in a frying pan and brown the turkey breasts on both sides. Remove the meat from the pan and make a large pocket in each breast with a sharp knife. Push half the stuffing into each pocket and secure with string or a cocktail stick. Place in a greased baking dish, cover and bake for about 30 minutes at Gas 4, 350 deg F, 180 deg C. Uncover the dish during the last 10 minutes to allow the meat to brown.
Serves 2.

SUMMER CHICKEN CASSEROLE

8 small chicken pieces
2–3 tablespoons seasoned flour
2–3 tablespoons corn oil
1 onion, peeled and finely chopped
1 clove garlic, crushed
2 ripe tomatoes, sliced
4 oz mushrooms, wiped and halved (110 g)
1 small green pepper, deseeded and sliced
1 pint chicken stock (600 ml)
1 tablespoon tomato purée
1 tablespoon fresh basil, chopped
1 sprig each thyme and rosemary
salt and freshly ground black pepper

Heat the oil in a large frying pan. Coat the chicken pieces in seasoned flour, then fry them in the oil, turning frequently, until they are browned on all sides. Remove from the pan and keep warm. Soften the onion and garlic in the same pan, then stir in the tomatoes, mushrooms and pepper and cook for a few minutes. Arrange half of these vegetables in the base of an ovenproof casserole, season with salt and pepper, place the chicken pieces on top, then put the rest of the vegetables over the chicken. Mix the tomato purée with the stock and pour into the casserole so that it covers the chicken pieces. Cover and cook for 1 hour 40 minutes at Gas 4, 350 deg F, 180 deg C. Add the herbs 15 minutes before the end of the cooking time. Top up with stock if necessary. Check the seasoning before serving. Serve hot with French beans and new potatoes.

TIPSY TURKEY

4 turkey breasts
2 tablespoons olive oil
1 oz butter (55 g)
12 juniper berries, crushed
3 fl oz red Vermouth (75 ml)
salt and freshly ground black pepper
2 tablespoons single cream

Slice each turkey breast diagonally into two or three neat pieces. Heat the oil and butter together in a frying pan, then gently cook the turkey in batches until brown on all sides. Remove and keep warm. Pour the Vermouth into the pan, stir in the juniper berries, and add a little salt and pepper. Allow to bubble up, then replace the turkey and cook for 10–15 minutes or until nice and tender. Take off the heat, strain the sauce, and stir in the cream. Reheat very gently. Serve with tiny new potatoes and a green vegetable.

TURKEY TIKKA

4 small turkey breasts, skinned and cut into strips
$\frac{1}{4}$ pint thick natural yogurt (150 ml)
juice of $\frac{1}{2}$ a lemon
1 teaspoon each chilli powder, ground cumin and coriander
1 clove garlic, crushed
1 inch piece root ginger, peeled and crushed (2.5 cm)
2 tablespoons tomato purée
1 onion, peeled and finely chopped
3 tablespoons corn or sunflower oil
salt and freshly ground black pepper

to serve:
1 lemon, cut into quarters
shredded lettuce

Place the prepared turkey in a shallow non-metal bowl. Mix together the yogurt, lemon juices, spices, garlic, ginger, tomato purée, and some salt and pepper. Pour over the turkey, mix well, and leave in a cool place for at least three hours. Turn occasionally if you remember. To cook, pour two tablespoons of oil on to a baking dish and add the onion. Place the turkey pieces on top. Cook at Gas 4, 350 deg F, 180 deg C, for about 25–30 minutes, basting with the rest of the oil half way through. (Alternatively, you can cook this dish under a very hot grill but it tends to be more time consuming and less reliable.) Serve hot or cold on a bed of shredded lettuce garnished with lemon quarters and accompanied by rice.

TURKEY WITH NUTS AND HONEY

1 fresh turkey, weighing about 10–12 lb (4.5–5.4 kg), plus giblets
2 oz butter (55 g)
2 tablespoons runny honey
2 oz bulghur wheat (55 g)
2 oz hazelnuts or walnuts, chopped (55 g)
grated zest and juice of $\frac{1}{2}$ a lemon
1 tablespoon each fresh parsley and chives, chopped
salt and freshly ground black pepper
2 teaspoons cornflour

Remove the giblets from the bird. Dry inside and out with kitchen paper. Pour boiling water over the bulghur wheat and leave to soak for a few minutes. Meanwhile, mix together the chopped nuts, lemon zest and juice, herbs, half the butter and some salt and pepper. Drain the bulghur wheat, squeezing out excess moisture, and mix into the nut mixture. Pack into the neck end of the turkey and secure the flap of skin with a skewer.

Rub the rest of the butter over the bird and wrap it loosely in foil. Bake at Gas 7, 425 deg F, 220 deg C for 15 minutes, then turn down the heat to Gas 3, 325 deg F, 170 deg C, and cook for another $2\frac{1}{2}$–3 hours. Uncover for the last half hour, turn up the heat, and baste frequently with the honey. Leave to rest for 15 minutes before carving.

To make gravy, simmer the giblets with some fresh herbs and peppercorns, strain, mix a little with the cornflour to make a smooth paste, and return paste and stock to the pan. Heat through for five minutes, and serve with the turkey.
Serves 6–8.

MEAT

Pork · Kidneys · Beef · Liver · Lamb · Sausage · Burgers

MEAT

Lots of people are eating less meat than they used to, for a variety of reasons. Cutting down on red meat or fatty meat is certainly a good thing, but with a family of four growing boys, I am not one of those who says we should do without this major source of protein altogether.

Butchers and supermarkets are responding to the decline in demand from a more discerning public by offering us meat from animals that have been reared more humanely, with less fat on it, and prepared for easy cooking.

If you are looking to cut down your family's intake of meat, try using less meat in a casserole and replacing the weight with button onions, mushrooms, or red kidney or butter beans. In a cottage pie, use lentils instead of some of the mince. Good both for wealth and health—and your family probably won't even notice!

Nevertheless, you can't beat a good rich beef casserole on a cold winter's evening, or a roast leg of lamb pierced with sweet and pungent garlic, or a springtime navarin of lamb casseroled with masses of tiny, tender vegetables.

Beef:
Beef and apple casserole
Beef and butter bean casserole
Beefburgers
Belgian carbonade (beef braised in ale)
Boeuf en daube (bacon-wrapped cubes of beef in wine)
Garlic beef and vegetable stir fry
Indian beef kebabs
Mexican beef tacos
Old-fashioned steak and kidney pudding
Lamb:
  Autumn lamb stew
  Lamb with rosemary and lemon
  Lancashire hotpot
  Navarin of lamb (springtime lamb casserole)
  Raan (spicy leg of lamb)
  Roast leg of lamb with garlic
  Rogan Josh (spicy lamb and tomato casserole)
  Spiced lamb kebabs

Stifado (Greek lamb stew)
Stir fried lamb with vegetables
Pork:
  Afelia (pork with red wine and coriander)
  Apple and cheese pork burgers
  Economical pork casserole
  Honey and ginger spare ribs
  Pork and cabbage bake
  Pork escalopes with lemon and tarragon
  Pork goulash
  Pork satay
  Pork with cider and apples
  Pork with green olives
  Sesame pork and bean sprout stir fry
Offal:
  Crispy liver with tartare sauce
  Faggots
  Italian liver
  Kidneys turbigo
  Liver Stroganoff

BEEF AND APPLE CASSEROLE

Do not worry when you discover that there is no stock, water, or booze in this recipe; it is not needed. The apples cook down with the onions and meat juices to make their own most delicious sauce.

2 lb shin of beef, trimmed of fat and cut into cubes (1 kg)
2 tablespoons plain flour seasoned with salt and pepper
2 tablespoons corn or sunflower oil
2 large cooking apples, peeled, cored and sliced
2 onions, peeled and thinly sliced
2 teaspoons fresh sage, chopped
salt and freshly ground black pepper

Toss the cubed meat in the seasoned flour. Heat the oil, then fry the beef in batches until it is browned on all sides. Place in layers with the apple and onion in a large casserole dish, seasoning with sage as you go. Cover tightly with buttered foil, which should just touch the meat, and then with a lid. Cook for 3 hours at Gas 1, 275 deg F, 140 deg C. Don't worry that this recipe contains no stock in the ingredients; the apples cook down to a pulp and combine to make a delicious gravy with the meat juices. Check the seasoning shortly before serving, and add more salt and pepper if needed. Serve with noodles and mixed vegetables.

BEEF AND BUTTER BEAN CASSEROLE

6 oz butter beans (175 g)
1 lb chuck steak, cubed (450 g)
2 oz butter (55 g)
1 medium onion, peeled and chopped
1 large clove garlic, crushed
1 large tomato, skinned and chopped
2 tablespoons tomato purée
1 teaspoon ground mixed spice
salt and freshly ground black pepper

Soak the beans overnight in plenty of cold water, then simmer in unsalted water for 20 minutes. Drain. Melt the butter in a flameproof casserole, then gently fry the onion and garlic for about ten minutes. Turn up the heat and fry the beef until brown on all sides. Add the tomato, tomato purée, beans and enough water to cover. Bring to the boil, add the mixed spice and some salt and pepper, then cover and transfer to the oven. Cook at Gas 3, 325 deg F, 170 deg C for about an hour. Check the seasoning 15 minutes before the end of the cooking time.

BEEFBURGERS

Home made beefburgers are much better than bought ones, and although they are fairly time-consuming to make, they can be prepared at some convenient point in the day and then stored in the fridge until needed.

>1 small onion, peeled and quartered
>4 oz smoked bacon (110 g)
>1¼ lb lean beef (575 g)
>1 tablespoon tomato purée
>1 tablespoon fresh parsley, chopped
>1 teaspoon fresh sage leaves, chopped
>salt and freshly ground black pepper

Place the onion, bacon and beef in the bowl of a food processor, and process until well blended. Add the tomato purée, herbs and seasoning and mix in. Turn out, and with wettened hands, shape the mixture into eight burgers. Chill them for about 30 minutes, then brush with oil and barbecue or grill for about 10 minutes, turning once. Serve in wholemeal buns with lettuce, sliced tomato, and relish. These burgers will freeze well; if cooking from frozen, allow a longer grilling time.
Makes 8.

BELGIAN CARBONADE
Beef braised in ale

2 lb lean stewing beef (1 kg)
3 small onions, peeled and thinly sliced
1 pint brown ale (600 ml)
¼ pint beef stock (150 ml)
2 tablespoons corn or sunflower oil
1 oz butter (25 g)
1 oz plain flour (25 g)

1 teaspoon sugar
5 or 6 slices French bread
2 tablespoons Dijon mustard
1 teaspoon dried mixed herbs, or
  a bunch of fresh herbs
salt and freshly ground black pepper

Heat the oil in a frying pan, then fry the beef in two or three batches until browned on all sides, keeping each batch warm. Add the onions to the frying pan and allow to soften. When just beginning to brown, remove the onions and layer them with the meat in an ovenproof casserole. Melt the butter in the frying pan and stir in the flour to make a smooth paste. Cook gently for two minutes, then gradually add the beer and stock, stirring well until you obtain a smooth sauce. Stir in the sugar and allow it to dissolve, then pour over the meat and onions. Season with salt and plenty of freshly ground black pepper, and add the dried herbs, if using. Cover and cook in the oven for 2½ hours at Gas 2, 300 deg F, 150 deg C. Add the fresh herbs, if using, 15 minutes before the end of the cooking time, and remove them before you add the bread and mustard crust. At the end of the cooking time, spread the slices of French bread with mustard, pop them, mustard-side down, on top of the meat, and brown under the grill.

BOEUF EN DAUBE PROVENCALE
Cubes of bacon-wrapped beef braised in wine

2 lb lean chuck steak in 2 inch (5 mm) cubes (1 kg)
12 rashers (approx) smoked streaky bacon
½ pint white wine (300 ml)
½ pint beef stock (300 ml)
1 tablespoon brandy
1 clove garlic, crushed
4 oz mushrooms, wiped (110 g)
1 small onion, peeled
2 tomatoes, peeled
4 oz black olives (110 g)
2 carrots, scrubbed
salt and freshly ground black pepper
a sprig of thyme
a bay leaf
6 parsley stalks
a sliver of orange peel

Cut the bacon rashers in half and use to wrap around each piece of steak. Now pack the little parcels into a non-metal bowl and cover with the wine and brandy. Leave to marinate for 24 hours. Next day, chop or slice the vegetables. Arrange the meat in an ovenproof casserole in alternating layers with the mushrooms, onions, tomatoes, olives and carrots. Tie the herbs and orange peel together and push into the middle. Season. Pour the marinade liquid over the meat and add enough beef stock to cover. Cover tightly and cook at Gas 1, 275 deg F, 140 deg C for 3 hours or so, until the meat is tender. Leave to go cold, skim off the fat, and re-heat for one hour at the same temperature when ready to eat.

GARLIC BEEF AND VEGETABLE STIR FRY

1 lb rump steak, cut into thin strips (450 g)
1 tablespoon sunflower oil
2 cloves garlic, crushed
1 leek, washed
1 red pepper, deseeded
½ a cucumber, seeds removed
6 oz Chinese leaves, washed (175 g)
2 tablespoons soy sauce
1 tablespoon dry sherry
1 teaspoon five spice powder

Slice the leek and red pepper as thinly as possible; chop the cucumber into small dice, and finely shred the Chinese cabbage leaves. Heat the oil in a wok or large frying pan until smoking hot, then add the beef and garlic, stirring continuously until brown. Remove the beef. Add the prepared vegetables and continue to stir fry for another two or three minutes. Stir in all the remaining ingredients, replace the beef, and stir fry for another minute. Serve with noodles or rice.

INDIAN BEEF KEBABS

1½ lb lean minced beef (675 g)
½ inch piece root ginger, peeled (1 cm)
1 onion, peeled and roughly chopped
2 fresh green chillis, deseeded and chopped
1 teaspoon mango chutney
2 tablespoons fresh coriander leaves, chopped
½ teaspoon poppy seeds
1 teaspoon each garam masala, chilli powder and ground cumin
salt and freshly ground black pepper
for the minty yogurt dip:
½ pint thick natural yogurt (300 ml)
¼ cucumber, finely chopped
2 tablespoons fresh mint, chopped
1 teaspoon ground cumin
a pinch of cayenne pepper
salt and pepper to taste

Using a food processor, process the root ginger, onion and chillis until the mixture is almost like a paste. If you do not have a food processor, chop the ingredients as finely as you can. Mix this with the rest of the kebab ingredients until well blended. Divide the mixture into 16 portions and shape each portion into a sausage. String them on eight skewers (bamboo skewers should be soaked in water beforehand to prevent them burning.) Place under a pre-heated grill and cook for 7–10 minutes, turning occasionally. Meanwhile, make the dip to serve with the kebabs: combine all the ingredients and chill before serving.
Serves 4, with rice, as a main course; 8 as a starter

MEXICAN BEEF TACOS

1 lb lean minced beef (450 g)
1 tablespoon malt vinegar
salt and freshly ground black pepper
½ teaspoon sugar
1 tablespoon sunflower oil
1 onion, peeled and finely chopped
1 clove garlic, crushed
1 green pepper, deseeded and chopped
2 dried chillis, chopped
¼ pint beef stock (150 ml)
2 tablespoons flaked almonds
7 oz can sweetcorn, drained (225 g)
3 tablespoons tomato purée
1 tablespoon cornflour
6–8 bought taco shells

Mix together the minced beef, vinegar, sugar and a little salt and plenty of pepper. Heat the oil in a large frying pan and lightly fry the onion, garlic, pepper and chillis. Add the minced beef and brown all over, stirring from time to time. Tip off any surplus fat that escapes. Add the beef stock, almonds, sweetcorn and tomato purée. Blend the cornflour with two tablespoons cold water, and stir in. Cover and simmer for 30 minutes, stirring now and then. Divide the mixture between the taco shells and serve hot, with a crunchy green salad.

OLD-FASHIONED STEAK AND KIDNEY PUDDING

for the dough:
8 oz self raising flour (225 g)
4 oz grated suet (110 g)
½ teaspoon salt

for the filling:
1 lb good steak and kidney in neat pieces (450 g)
1 tablespoon seasoned flour
1 stock cube
1 onion, peeled and chopped
1 tablespoon fresh herbs, chopped, or 2 teaspoons mixed dried herbs

Sift the flour, mix it with the suet, and add enough water to make a soft but not sticky dough. Press the dough lightly on a floured board until it is about ¼ inch (½ cm) thick. Grease a pudding basin and line it with three quarters of the dough. Crumble the stock cube into the bottom of the basin, then roll the meat in the seasoned flour before adding it to the basin together with the herbs and onion. Cover with water. Press out the rest of the dough to form a lid; wet the edges and press it down well to make sure it sticks. Cover with a lid (if your basin has one) or greaseproof paper tied down well. Place in a pan of boiling water and steam for at least three hours, topping the pan up with more boiling water as needed. Serve with green vegetables.

LAMB DISHES

AUTUMN LAMB STEW

1 tablespoon corn or sunflower oil
2 lb stewing lamb (1 kg)
1 large onion, peeled and chopped
1 clove garlic, crushed
2 teaspoons sugar
1 tablespoon flour
1 pint stock (600 ml)
1 sprig each rosemary and thyme
1 bay leaf, crushed
12 small potatoes, scrubbed
12 small carrots, scrubbed
6 small turnips, scrubbed and halved
8 oz runner beans, trimmed and chopped (225 g)
salt and freshly ground black pepper

Trim the lamb of fat and cut into neat pieces. Heat the oil in a flameproof casserole, then soften the onion and garlic. Now add the lamb, turn up the heat, and brown the meat all over. Stir in the flour and sugar, cook for a minute or two, then pour in about three quarters of the stock. Add the herbs, cover and place in the oven at Gas 3, 325 deg F, 170 deg C, and cook for an hour. Now add the potatoes, carrots and turnips, add some salt and pepper and the remaining stock if needed to cover the vegetables, and cook for another hour. Add the chopped runner beans 20 minutes before the end of the cooking time. Remove the herbs before serving.

LAMB WITH ROSEMARY AND LEMON

3 lb (approx) shoulder of lamb, boned and rolled (1.4 kg)
2–3 sprigs rosemary
1 garlic clove, cut into thin slivers

for the stuffing:
grated zest of a lemon
3–4 sprigs rosemary
1 clove garlic, crushed
4 tablespoons fresh breadcrumbs
salt and freshly ground black pepper
1 small egg

Blanch the rosemary for a few minutes in boiling water, strip off the leaves, and chop them finely. Mix with the rest of the stuffing ingredients, adding enough egg to bind it all together. Unroll the meat, place the stuffing mixture in the middle, and roll up again, tying securely. Don't overfill; if there is too much stuffing, make tiny balls and cook them with the meat for half an hour. Make slits in the flesh of the lamb and insert tiny sprigs of rosemary and slivers of garlic. Place the meat on a rack above a tin, to catch the juices, and cook for $2-2\frac{1}{4}$ hours at Gas 4, 350 deg F, 180 deg C. Allow the joint to rest in a warm place for 15 minutes before carving thinly. Use the skimmed tin juices and the juices in the foil to make gravy, perhaps adding a teaspoon or two of redcurrant jelly.

LANCASHIRE HOTPOT

dripping or oil for frying
2 lb lean neck of lamb (1 kg)
4 oz lambs' kidneys, rinsed, cored and quartered (110 g)
3 onions, peeled and sliced
1 large turnip, scrubbed and sliced
2–3 carrots, scrubbed and chopped
1 tablespoon flour

1 pint hot stock (600 ml)
1 teaspoon Worcester sauce
1 bay leaf, crushed
1 sprig each rosemary and thyme
2 lb potatoes, scrubbed and sliced (1 kg)
salt and freshly ground black pepper
a little butter

Slice the lamb into neat, fairly large pieces and heat the oil or dripping in a frying pan. Fry the meat in batches until it is well browned on all sides. Brown the kidneys too. Keep the meat warm in a large, wide casserole. Add the onions to the frying pan and cook gently until golden brown. Transfer to the casserole, together with the turnip and carrots. Now sprinkle the flour into the frying pan, scraping well to get all the bits up, and then pour in the stock and Worcester sauce. Stir until the liquid is blended, and then pour it into the casserole. Tuck in the herbs and season with salt and pepper. Arrange the potato slices on top, overlapping in an attractive pattern. Add a little more seasoning as you go, dot with flecks of butter, cover with a lid or pleated foil and bake for $1\frac{1}{2}$ hours at Gas 3, 325 deg F, 170 deg C, then remove the lid and continue cooking for 40–50 minutes to allow the potatoes to brown. Finish off under the grill to get the spuds really crisp. Serve hot with cabbage or green beans.

NAVARIN OF LAMB
Lamb casserole with spring vegetables

2 lb lean lamb (1 kg)
3 tablespoons corn or sunflower oil
2 teaspoons sugar
2 tablespoons plain flour
4 tomatoes, chopped
1 garlic clove, crushed
1 sprig each rosemary and thyme

1 bay leaf, crushed
2 medium onions, peeled and chopped
12 baby carrots, scrubbed
12 small new potatoes, scrubbed
4 small turnips, scrubbed and quartered
4 oz peas, shelled weight (110 g)
salt and freshly ground black pepper

Heat the oil in a large flameproof casserole and brown the lamb on all sides. Stir in the sugar and allow to brown. Sprinkle in the flour, cook for two minutes, then add enough water just to cover the meat. Season and bring to the boil, stirring, then add the tomatoes, garlic and herbs. Cover and cook gently at Gas 2, 300 deg F, 150 deg C for an hour. Now add the prepared onions, carrots, potatoes and turnips and cook for another $1\frac{1}{4}$ hours. Add the peas 25 minutes before the end of the cooking time, and check the seasoning. Remove the herbs, and serve sprinkled with fresh chopped parsley.

RAAN
Spicy leg of lamb

1 leg of lamb, about 4 lb (1.8 kg)
2–3 onions, peeled and finely chopped
4 cloves garlic, crushed
½ pint natural yogurt (300 ml)
1 oz ground almonds (25 g)
2 inch piece root ginger, peeled and finely grated (5 cm)
2 tablespoons tomato purée
juice of 1 lemon
2 teaspoons each turmeric and chilli powder
1 teaspoon each ground cumin, coriander, and black pepper

to garnish:
2 oz blanched almonds (55 g)

With a sharp knife, carefully remove all the skin and as much fat as possible from the lamb, and make several deep gashes into the flesh. Place all the remaining ingredients, apart from the blanched almonds, in the bowl of a food processor, and blend until smooth. Place the lamb in a neat-fitting non-metal bowl, then spread the yogurt and onion mixture over it, pushing well into the gashes. Cover with clingfilm, foil or a lid and leave to marinate in the fridge for 12–36 hours (the longer you can leave it, the more pronounced the flavours will be.) To cook, remove the meat and weigh, then wrap loosely in foil, and roast at Gas 5, 375 deg F, 190 deg C for 30 minutes to the 1 lb (450 g). 30 minutes before the end of the cooking time, open up the foil and sprinkle the almonds over the joint.
Serves 6–8.

ROAST LEG OF LAMB WITH GARLIC

1 leg of lamb weighing approx 5 lb (2.2 kg)
2 fat cloves garlic
4 small sprigs rosemary
2 tablespoons redcurrant or rosemary jelly
1 tablespoon cornflour

With a sharp knife, make little cuts all over the surface of the lamb. Peel the garlic and cut it into slivers, and put a little sliver into each cut. Insert the sprigs of rosemary into the flesh in the same way. Brush with the jelly. Place the lamb on a rack over a tray to catch the fat, and roast in a pre-heated oven at Gas 6, 400 deg F, 200 deg C, for 20 minutes, then reduce the heat to Gas 4, 350 deg F, 180 deg C for 30 minutes to the 1 lb (450 g). Leave the meat to rest in a warm place for 10 minutes or so before carving into thick slices. Meanwhile, make gravy from the juices in the pan, having first tipped off any fat, stirring in a little extra redcurrant or rosemary jelly and thickening it up with a tablespoon of cornflour.

ROGAN JOSH
Spicy lamb and tomato casserole

$1\frac{1}{2}$ lb lean lamb, cubed (675 g)
2 tablespoons corn or sunflower oil
2 onions, peeled and finely chopped
2 cloves garlic, crushed
$\frac{1}{2}$ teaspoon each ground ginger and cayenne pepper
$\frac{1}{4}$ teaspoon ground cinnamon
1 teaspoon ground coriander
2 teaspoons ground cumin
3 teaspoons paprika
2 cardamon pods, crushed
$\frac{1}{2}$ teaspoon sugar
salt and freshly ground black pepper
14 oz can chopped tomatoes (400 g)
$\frac{1}{4}$ pint water (150 ml)

Heat the oil in a large pan, deep frying pan, or flameproof casserole, and brown the meat on all sides. Remove the meat from the pan and keep warm. Add the onion and garlic and cook until soft. Now stir in the spices, sugar, salt and black pepper, cook for one minute, then return the meat to the pan. Stir in the tomatoes and the water. Cover and cook gently for an hour, stirring occasionally. Remove the lid and allow to simmer uncovered for another 30 minutes or so until the sauce thickens and the lamb is tender. Serve with rice and a vegetable curry.

SPICED LAMB KEBABS

8 oz lamb fillet, cubed (225 g)
4 tablespoons thick plain yogurt
$1\frac{1}{2}$ tablespoons lemon juice
1 inch piece fresh root ginger, peeled and finely grated (2.5 cm)
1 small green chilli, deseeded and finely chopped
1 clove garlic, crushed
1 teaspoon ground cumin
$\frac{1}{2}$ teaspoon each ground coriander and cayenne pepper
salt and freshly ground black pepper

Place the lamb in a large non-metal bowl. Mix together the yogurt, lemon juice, ginger, chilli, garlic, cumin, coriander, cayenne, salt and pepper in a large jug or bowl, and pour over the lamb. Mix meat and marinade together well, then leave in the fridge overnight or for at least three or four hours. Turn from time to time. When ready to cook, remove the meat from the marinade and thread on to skewers. Brush with oil, and place under a hot grill or on the barbecue, turning when brown and brushing with more oil. Serve hot, with rice and thick slices of lemon.

STIFADO
Greek lamb goulash

1½ lb lean lamb (700 g)
2 tablespoons olive oil
14 oz can tomatoes (400 g)
1 lb shallots, peeled (450 g)
1 teaspoon sugar
salt and freshly ground black pepper
grated rind and juice of ½ a lemon
3 whole cloves
1 inch piece cinnamon stick (2.5 cm)
8 fl oz red wine (250 ml)
2 sprigs fresh rosemary

Trim the lamb of fat and cut into 1 inch (2.5 cm) cubes. Heat the oil in a flameproof casserole, then add the lamb, browning it on all sides. Add all the other ingredients except the rosemary. Cover, reduce the heat to a gentle simmer, and cook for 1½ hours. Take off the lid and add the rosemary. Turn up the heat a little to allow the sauce to thicken, and cook for another 15 minutes. (As with most dishes of this type, it tastes even better prepared the day before and then heated through for an hour before eating.)

STIR FRIED LAMB WITH VEGETABLES

1 lb lamb steaks, sliced thinly (450 g)
1 tablespoon sunflower oil
1 clove garlic, crushed
6–8 spring onions
3 carrots, scrubbed
2–3 tender sticks celery, washed
3 young courgettes, washed
2–4 oz white cabbage, washed (50–100 g)
salt and freshly ground black pepper
2 teaspoons Worcester sauce
1 tablespoon soy sauce
4 tablespoons apple juice

Slice all the vegetables into matchsticks or very thin slices before starting to cook. Shred the cabbage finely. Heat the oil in a wok or large frying pan and fry the lamb for five or six minutes, until browned and cooked through. Remove from the pan and keep warm. Add the garlic, onions, carrots, celery and courgettes to the pan and continue to stir fry for a minute or two, keeping the heat up and stirring all the time. Add plenty of seasoning, the Worcester sauce, soy sauce and apple juice and return the lamb to the pan. Cook for two or three minutes, stirring frequently and serve at once with freshly-boiled noodles or rice.

PORK DISHES

AFELIA
Pork with wine and coriander

2 tablespoons olive oil
2 lb lean pork, cut into $\frac{1}{2}$ inch (1 cm) cubes (1 kg)
about $\frac{1}{2}$ pint robust dry red wine (300 ml)
4 oz button mushrooms, wiped and sliced (110 g)
1 tablespoon coriander seeds
salt and freshly ground black pepper

Heat the oil in a large frying pan, then brown the pork on all sides, stirring well. Pour in the wine. Let it bubble up, then turn down the heat and cover the pan. Simmer gently for 10–15 minutes, then add the sliced mushrooms and stir. Replace the lid and cook for another five minutes or so. If the pan is dry, add another splash of wine; the juices should nearly all have been absorbed by the end of the cooking time. Stir in the finely crushed coriander seeds (ready ground coriander doesn't work as well), add some salt and pepper, and cook for another five minutes. Serve hot with rice and a crisp green vegetable.

APPLE AND CHEESE PORK BURGERS

1 lb lean pork, minced (450 g)
1 onion, peeled and finely chopped
1 tablespoon fresh sage and parsley
salt and freshly ground black pepper
1 small egg, beaten
plain flour, for shaping

for the filling:
1 small eating apple, peeled, cored and sliced into four rings
2 oz Sage Derby or Cheddar cheese, chopped small (55 g)
1 tablespoon vegetable oil

Mix together the meat, onion, herbs, seasoning and egg. With floured hands, shape the mixture into eight rounds and flatten. Place a slice of apple and a tablespoon of the cheese on four of the burger rounds. Place another burger round on top and mould around the apple and cheese. Pinch the edges to seal. Shape into four large burgers. Brush lightly with oil, and grill for 5–7 minutes on each side. Serve with a crisp salad and sesame seed bun.

ECONOMICAL PORK CASSEROLE

2–3 lb belly pork (1–1.5 kg)
1 bay leaf, crushed
1 sprig thyme
6 sage leaves
6 black peppercorns
1 clove garlic, crushed
1 tablespoon sunflower oil

1 medium onion, peeled and chopped
2 sticks celery, washed and chopped
4 oz red lentils (110 g)
2–3 carrots, washed and chopped
4–6 tomatoes, chopped
1 stock cube

The day before you plan to eat the dish, cut up the belly pork into 1 inch (2.5 cm) pieces, removing all the rind and as much fat as you can. Place the meat in a pan with the herbs, peppercorns and garlic, and cover with water. Bring to the boil, skim, then cover and simmer gently for 1½ hours. Allow to cool a little, then strain the meat, reserving the cooking liquor in a jug or bowl. Remove the herbs, peppercorns and garlic and discard, and, when the meat is cold, trim off any fat. Keep meat and stock in the fridge overnight. Next day, heat the oil in an ovenproof casserole dish and soften the onion and celery. Add the lentils, stir around a little, then add the carrots, tomatoes and pork. Crumble in the stock cube and season with salt and pepper. Take off the layer of fat that will have solidified on top of the reserved cooking liquor, and pour in enough liquid to cover the contents of the casserole. Cover and cook in the oven for 1½ hours at Gas 4, 350 deg F, 180 deg C. Serve with baked potatoes.

HONEY AND GINGER SPARE RIBS

1½ lb spare ribs (675 g)
2 tablespoons honey
2 tablespoons ginger syrup (from a jar of stem ginger)
1 tablespoon vinegar
¼ pint medium or dry cider (150 ml)
2 tablespoons rich soy sauce
½ inch piece root ginger, peeled and grated (1 cm)
salt and freshly ground black pepper

If the ribs look fatty, place them in boiling water for 20 minutes to take off some of the fat; drain well and pat dry on kitchen paper. Place the ribs in a shallow dish. Whisk all the other ingredients together and pour over the meat. Place in the fridge and leave to marinate for about three hours, turning occasionally. When ready to cook, place the ribs in a shallow baking dish, pour the marinade over, and bake for one hour at Gas 6, 400 deg F, 200 deg C, turning now and then. Serve the ribs with the sauce poured over—it should be quite thick after cooking, but if not, make a little cornflour paste and use to thicken. Serve with rice and stir fried vegetables. Serves 2–3.

PORK AND CABBAGE BAKE

1 lb lean casserole pork, cubed (450 g)
1 small cabbage
1 tablespoon sunflower oil
1 onion, peeled and finely chopped
1 tablespoon plain flour
1 teaspoon ground coriander
$\frac{1}{2}$ pint medium cider (300 ml)
8 baby carrots, scrubbed
salt and freshly ground black pepper
2 oz brown breadcrumbs (55 g)
2 oz plain wholemeal flour (55 g)
2 oz margarine or butter (55 g)
2 oz farmhouse Cheddar, grated (55 g)

Heat the oil in a frying pan or flameproof casserole and soften the onion. Shred the cabbage finely, discarding stalk and tough outer leaves, and put on to cook in a little lightly salted boiling water. Add the pork to the onions, turn up the heat, and brown the meat on all sides. Now stir in the tablespoon of flour and the ground coriander, cook for a minute, then add the cider, carrots, and some salt and pepper. Simmer, covered, for half an hour. When the cabbage is cooked but not soggy, drain it well and place in the base of a shallow ovenproof dish. When the pork and carrots are tender, layer them and their sauce on top of the cabbage. Whizz up the remaining ingredients in a food processor, adding a little salt and pepper, and then sprinkle over the meat. Bake for 30 minutes in the oven at Gas 5, 375 deg F, 190 deg C or until the top is crispy.

PORK ESCALOPES WITH LEMON AND TARRAGON

1 lb pork fillet (450 g)
1 egg, beaten
4 oz dry breadcrumbs (110 g)
grated zest of a lemon
2 teaspoons fresh tarragon, chopped
salt and freshly ground black pepper
2–3 tablespoons corn or sunflower oil

to serve:
lemon wedges

Slice the pork fillet into pieces about $\frac{1}{4}$ inch (0.5 cm) thick. Bash with a meat hammer or rolling pin to flatten them. Combine the breadcrumbs with the lemon zest, tarragon and seasoning in a bowl. Coat each pork slice with beaten egg, then dip in breadcrumbs and cover both sides. I find this easiest to do by spearing each escalope on the prongs of a fork. Heat the oil until very hot in a large frying pan and fry each breadcrumbed escalope for five minutes on each side or until golden brown. Serve with lemon wedges.
Serves 2–3.

PORK GOULASH

2 tablespoons sunflower oil
4 pork steaks
1 large onion, peeled and sliced
2 tablespoons plain wholewheat flour
1 heaped tablespoon paprika
1 lb tin Italian tomatoes (400 g)
1 tablespoon tomato purée
¾ pint chicken stock (450 ml)
1 red pepper, deseeded and sliced
¼ pint natural yogurt (150 ml)

Cut the pork into good-sized pieces. Heat the oil in a large frying pan and fry the pork until browned on all sides. Transfer to an ovenproof casserole and keep warm. Fry the onions in the same frying pan until they collapse, then add the flour and paprika, and cook for one minute, stirring continuously. Now add the tomatoes and their juice, and the tomato purée. Break up the tomatoes with a spoon and scrape up all the bits stuck to the bottom of the pan. Pour over the meat. Add enough chicken stock to cover the meat, then put on a lid and cook in a pre-heated oven at Gas 4, 350 deg F, 180 deg C for one hour, or until the meat is tender. Add the red pepper to the casserole 10 minutes before the end of the cooking time. Stir in the yogurt, pop back in the oven for a few minutes, then serve, sprinkled with more paprika.

PORK SATAY WITH PEANUT SAUCE

for the satay (kebabs):
8 oz chump chops or steak from a shoulder or leg of pork (225 g)
1 tablespoon lemon juice
1 tablespoon soy sauce
1 clove garlic, crushed

for the sauce:
6 tablespoons water
2 tablespoons crunchy peanut butter
1 tablespoon soy sauce
1 tablespoon lemon juice
a dash of chilli sauce

to serve:
shredded lettuce
½ a lemon, sliced

Cut the pork into small pieces and place in a bowl. Mix together the lemon juice, soy sauce and garlic, pour over the pork, and leave to stand in a cool place for several hours. When ready to serve, thread the pork on to four skewers and place on a baking tray under a hot grill. Pour over any leftover marinade. Grill for four minutes, then turn over and cook for another four minutes. Meanwhile, make the peanut sauce: add the water to the peanut butter, beating in one tablespoon at a time until smooth. Add the rest of the sauce ingredients. Serve in a small bowl with the satay, which may be served hot or cold, on a bed of shredded lettuce and garnished with lemon slices.
Serves 2.

PORK WITH CIDER AND APPLES

1 lb casserole pork, cubed (450 g)
2 tablespoons corn or sunflower oil
1 onion, peeled and chopped
1 tablespoon fresh sage, chopped, or 1 teaspoon dried sage
1 large cooking apple, peeled, cored and sliced
2 oz brown breadcrumbs (55 g)
$\frac{1}{4}$ pint dry or medium cider (150 ml)
salt and freshly ground black pepper

Heat the oil in a flameproof casserole and brown the meat on all sides. Transfer to a plate and keep warm. Soften the onion in the casserole, then replace the pork, add the sage and some salt and pepper. Pour in enough cider to cover, arrange the apples on top, and then sprinkle with breadcrumbs. Cover and bake for one hour at Gas 4, 350 deg F, 180 deg C, then remove the lid and cook for another 15 minutes to crisp up the breadcrumbs.
Serves 3–4.

PORK WITH GREEN OLIVES

$1\frac{1}{2}$ lb pork fillet (675 g)
1 red onion, peeled and thinly sliced
1 small red pepper, deseeded and cut into thin rings
1 clove garlic, crushed
2 or 3 tablespoons olive oil
2 tablespoons plain flour
$\frac{1}{2}$ pint red wine (300 ml)
4 tomatoes, peeled and chopped, or a small tin of Italian tomatoes
16 green olives, halved and stoned
2 tablespoons fresh basil, chopped
salt and freshly ground black pepper

Slice the pork diagonally into pieces about $\frac{1}{2}$ inch (1 cm) thick. Heat the oil in a frying pan and quickly fry the pork until brown on all sides. Transfer to an ovenproof casserole and keep warm while you soften the onion, garlic and red pepper in the frying pan. Stir in the flour and cook for one minute. Pour in the wine, bring to the boil, then turn down the heat and simmer for a couple of minutes, then transfer to the casserole. Add the tomatoes to the casserole, and season. Cover and bake at Gas 2, 300 deg F, 150 deg C for 40–50 minutes. Add the olives and basil and cook for further 20 minutes. Serve with rice.
Serves 3–4.

SESAME PORK AND BEAN SPROUT STIR FRY

1½ lb pork fillet, cut into thin strips (700 g)
2–3 tablespoons sesame oil
½ a green pepper, deseeded and cut into strips
½ a red pepper, deseeded and cut into strips
1 carrot, scrubbed and chopped into matchsticks
white of a leek, scrubbed and finely sliced
6 oz mushrooms, wiped and finely sliced (175 g)
8 oz beansprouts, rinsed and dried (225 g)
1 tablespoon dark brown sugar
2 tablespoons sesame seeds

Heat two tablespoons of the oil in a wok or a very large frying pan until smoking hot. Tip in the sliced pork fillet and fry, stirring all the time, until browned on all sides, and cooked through. Transfer to a warmed plate and keep warm. Add the extra oil to the wok or pan if necessary, then add the peppers and carrot and stir fry for two or three minutes. Add the leek and mushrooms and stir fry for another two minutes. Tip in the bean sprouts and stir fry for two more minutes. Replace the pork in the pan. Whisk the sugar and soy sauce together, pour into the pan, and stir well. Serve immediately, sprinkled with the sesame seeds and accompanied by plain boiled rice.

OFFAL

CRISPY LIVER WITH TARTARE SAUCE

6 oz plain flour (175 g)
salt and freshly ground black pepper
1 lb lamb's liver, thinly sliced (450 g)
1 egg
¼ pint milk (150 ml)
oil for deep frying
¼ pint bought mayonnaise (150 ml)
2 tablespoons fresh parsley, chopped
2 tablespoons capers
4 pickled gherkins, drained and chopped small
grated zest and juice of 1 lemon

Mix about 2 oz (55 g) of the flour with some salt and pepper, and coat the thinly sliced liver in it. Sift the rest of the flour with a little salt into a bowl, make a well in the centre, add the egg and milk, and gradually work the mixture together until you have a smooth thick batter. Dip the liver in the batter. Heat the oil in a deep frying pan to 350 deg F, 180 deg C, or until a cube of bread browns in 30 seconds. Deep fry the liver a few pieces at a time until golden and crispy; this will take four or five minutes for each piece. Keep the cooked liver warm on a plate lined with kitchen paper in the oven. To make the sauce, combine the rest of the ingredients, adding enough lemon juice to reach the desired consistency. Serve with wedges of lemon and a crisp salad.

FAGGOTS

1 lb fresh pig's liver, roughly chopped (450 g)
12 oz unsalted belly pork, roughly chopped (350 g)
1 small onion, peeled and roughly chopped
1 teaspoon fresh sage leaves, finely chopped
½ teaspoon fresh thyme leaves
½ teaspoon freshly grated nutmeg
4 oz breadcrumbs (110 g)
salt and freshly ground black pepper

Cook the liver, pork and onion in a little water for 30 minutes. Drain, mince the meats and onion coarsely, mix together, then add all the other ingredients and mix well. Spread the mixture in a medium-sized roasting tin to a depth of about 1 inch (2.5 cm). Cover with buttered greaseproof paper. Cook at Gas 6, 400 deg F, 200 deg C for 40 minutes, marking the faggots into squares after 15 minutes. After 30 minutes, drain off the juices. Serve with dried marrowfat peas, soaked, and then cooked for 1½ hours to a mush.

ITALIAN LIVER

12 oz fresh lamb's liver (350 g)
2 tablespoons corn or sunflower oil
1 oz plain flour (25 g)
3 medium onions, peeled and thinly sliced
¼ pint beef stock (150 ml)
½ pint milk (300 ml)
2 level tablespoons tomato purée
¼ teaspoon each dried oregano, thyme and rosemary
2 tablespoons double cream (optional)
1 tablespoon fresh parsley, chopped
salt and freshly ground black pepper

Heat the oil in a frying pan and, while it is heating, cut the liver into small pieces and coat well in the flour seasoned with some salt and pepper. Brown the liver on all sides, then remove from the pan and keep warm on a plate. Now fry the onions fairly gently in the same pan until they are soft, then stir in the stock, milk, tomato purée, herbs and a little more salt and pepper. Bring to the boil, stirring all the time. Replace the liver, cover the pan, and cook gently for 10–15 minutes until the liver is tender. Check the seasoning. Place the liver and sauce on a hot serving dish, spoon the cream over if using, and sprinkle the chopped parsley on top. Serve with creamy mashed potato.

KIDNEYS TURBIGO

8 lamb's kidneys, skinned, cored and halved
2 tablespoons sunflower oil
12 chipolata sausages, twisted in half, or 24 cocktail sausages
12 button onions, peeled
8 oz button mushrooms, wiped (225 g)
4 teaspoons plain flour
¼ pint beef stock (150 ml)
4 tablespoons dry sherry
salt and freshly ground black pepper

to garnish:
fresh parsley, finely chopped

Heat the oil in a frying pan, then fry the kidneys to seal, and remove from the pan. Add the chipolatas to the pan and fry until browned all over. Remove from the pan and keep warm. Fry the onions in the same pan until golden brown, then add the mushrooms and continue cooking for a couple of minutes. Stir in the flour and cook for one minute, then gradually add the stock, stirring until it browns and thickens. Add the sherry and seasoning and return the kidneys and chipolatas to the pan. Cover the pan and simmer gently for 20–25 minutes until tender. Sprinkle liberally with fresh parsley, and serve with rice or pasta.

LIVER STROGANOFF

A poor man's Stroganoff this, and also a good way to get children to eat liver!

1 lb lamb's liver, cut into very thin strips (450 g)
1 red onion, peeled and chopped
3 tablespoons olive oil
1 tablespoon fresh herbs, such as parsley, thyme, tarragon and/or oregano, chopped
$\frac{1}{4}$ teaspoon freshly grated nutmeg
salt and freshly ground black pepper
1 tablespoon soy sauce
$\frac{1}{2}$ pint sour cream (300 ml)

Heat the oil in a large frying pan and soften the onion. Add the liver, and brown it on all sides. Add the herbs, nutmeg, seasoning, and soy sauce, and cook very gently until the liver is cooked—this will only take a few minutes. Stir in the sour cream away from the heat, then put back on the hob and heat through very gently. Serve with rice or noodles and a green salad.

PASTA · BEANS & RICE

Aduki beans · Lentils · Spaghetti · Ravioli · Risotto

PASTA, BEANS AND RICE

Vegetarian cookery has a lot to recommend it, not least because it's so imaginative. Many of the recipes in these pages were inspired by vegetarian cookbooks, but you don't have to be a "veggie" to enjoy them.

As well as being good for you, beans and rice are also cheap, and make excellent subjects for experiments in the kitchen. As long as you soak and cook beans properly, you can't really go wrong, and, even if you do, you won't make a really expensive mistake.

Tinned beans are easy and quick to deal with, but if you're really thrifty, dried beans are much cheaper. Remember to soak red kidney beans for 12 hours and then boil hard for at least ten minutes before starting to cook them.

Pasta is a terrific standby for the busy cook. My children love pasta shapes simply tossed in butter and a few herbs and topped with grated cheese, and we all adore spaghetti bolognaise and lasagne, eaten with a huge mixed salad.

I'm not really a convert to wholemeal pasta and wholegrain rice; if I feel like eating cardboard I gnaw cereal packets. However, in some recipes, a mixture of wholegrain and refined pasta or rice works reasonably well.

Beans and lentils:
  Aduki bean casserole
  Boston baked beans
  Lentil and mushroom bake
  Lentil casserole
  Mixed bean salad
  Spicy bean and pepper goulash
  Vegetarian cassoulet
  Vegetarian chilli
  Vegetarian cottage pie
Pasta:
  Macaroni carbonara
  Pasta Niçoise
  Pasta with asparagus
  Pasta with mushrooms
  Pasta with pork and peas
  Rigatoni with chicken livers
  Tagliatelle turkey
  Vegetable tagliatelle

Rice:
  Baked rice pilaff
  Brown rice pilaff
  Green risotto
  Ham, chicken and mushroom risotto
  Kedgeree
  Rice and lentil bake
  Rice, bean sprouts and sweetcorn salad
  Rice with pistachio nuts

BEANS AND LENTILS

ADUKI BEAN CASSEROLE

12 oz dried aduki beans (350 g)
2 onions, peeled and chopped
2 tablespoons sunflower oil
2 carrots, scrubbed and chopped
2 celery stalks, scrubbed and chopped
2 cloves garlic, crushed
1 lb smoked bacon (450 g)
1 lb tomatoes (450 g)

4 oz mushrooms, wiped and sliced (110 g)
1 teaspoon tomato purée
1 bay leaf, crushed
1 sprig thyme
freshly ground black pepper

to garnish:
fresh parsley, chopped

Soak the beans overnight in cold water. Next day, drain them, place in a pan and cover with clean cold water. Do not add salt. Bring to the boil, turn down the heat, cover and simmer for an hour. Heat the oven to Gas 4, 350 deg F, 180 deg C. Drain the beans and reserve about $\frac{3}{4}$ pint (450 ml) of the cooking liquid. Heat the oil in a flameproof casserole and fry the onions for about ten minutes. Add the carrots, celery and garlic and fry for a few more minutes. Dice the bacon, and skin and chop the tomatoes (when tomatoes are expensive, use a tin of peeled Italian tomatoes and their juices.) Add bacon, tomatoes and mushrooms to the pan. Stir well, then add the tomato purée, bay leaf, thyme, soaked beans and cooking liquor. Season with plenty of black pepper—salt is unnecessary because it will be contained in the bacon. Cover and cook in the oven for $1\frac{1}{2}$ hours until the beans are soft. Sprinkle with the parsley before serving.

BOSTON BAKED BEANS

10 oz dried haricot beans (275 g)
1 tablespoon corn or sunflower oil
2 red onions, peeled and chopped
1 tablespoon treacle
$\frac{1}{4}$ pint tomato juice (150 ml)
2 tablespoons tomato purée
1 tablespoon dark brown sugar
1 teaspoon English mustard powder
$\frac{1}{2}$ pint beef stock (300 ml)

Soak the beans overnight in plenty of cold water. Next day, drain them, then place in a large saucepan, cover with boiling water, and cook for half an hour. Drain. Towards the end of this time, heat the oil in a flameproof casserole, then sauté the onions until soft. Stir in the rest of the ingredients and take off the heat. Add the drained beans, cover, and bake in the oven at Gas 1, 275 deg F, 140 deg C for $2\frac{1}{2}$–3 hours, stirring now and then to prevent sticking. The beans should be nice and tender at the end of the cooking time and the sauce syrupy.

LENTIL AND MUSHROOM BAKE

8 oz red lentils (225 g)
1 oz butter (25 g)
1 tablespoon olive oil
1 clove garlic, crushed
1 large onion, peeled and finely chopped
2 oz mushrooms, wiped and sliced (55 g)
4 oz farmhouse Cheddar, grated (110 g)
2 oz walnuts, roughly chopped (55 g)
1 tablespoon fresh parsley, chopped
1 oz wholemeal breadcrumbs (25 g)
1 egg, beaten
salt and freshly ground black pepper

Simmer the lentils in $\frac{3}{4}$ pint of water (450 ml) until all the water is absorbed and the lentils are soft. This will take about 10–20 minutes; it rather depends on the age of your lentils. Meanwhile, melt the butter and olive oil together in a frying pan and soften the onion and garlic, allowing the onion to brown but not to burn. Add the sliced mushrooms and cook for a few more minutes, stirring so that they are well coated in the oil. Take the pan off the heat and transfer its contents to a large bowl. Add the lentils, cheese, walnuts, parsley, breadcrumbs, egg, and some salt and freshly ground black pepper. Mix well. Press the mixture into a greased baking dish about 9 inches (23 cm) square and at least 1 inch (2.5 cm) deep, and bake at Gas 5, 375 deg F, 190 deg C, for about 30 minutes. Serve hot or cold, cut into slices, with a green salad and tomatoes.

ves 4–6.

LENTIL CASSEROLE

2 tablespoons sunflower oil
1 onion, peeled
1 clove garlic, crushed
2 carrots, scrubbed
2 large potatoes, scrubbed
8 oz green or brown lentils (225 g)

14 oz can Italian tomatoes (400 g)
2 tablespoons tomato purée
$\frac{1}{2}$ pint vegetable stock (300 ml)
2 tablespoons fresh herbs, chopped
salt and freshly ground black pepper

Chop the vegetables into bite-sized pieces. Heat the oil in a frying pan and gently fry the onion, garlic, carrot and potatoes for 10–15 minutes, stirring now and then. Rinse the lentils in cold water, then add them to the frying pan with the tomatoes and their juice, tomato purée, stock, a little salt and plenty of pepper. Bring the lentils and vegetables to the boil, then turn down the heat, cover and simmer for about 30 minutes, or until everything is tender. Add the herbs ten minutes before the end of the cooking time. Stir occasionally, and add more stock or water if necessary to prevent sticking, but the end result should not be runny. Serve piping hot.

MIXED BEAN SALAD

2 oz each red kidney, haricot and aduki beans (55 g each)
6 tablespoons olive oil
2 tablespoons white wine vinegar or lemon juice
½ teaspoon sugar
½ teaspoon Dijon mustard
salt and freshly ground black pepper
1 tablespoon fresh chopped parsley, coriander or basil (or a mixture)
1 small red onion, peeled and thinly sliced

Soak the beans separately overnight in plenty of cold water. Next day, drain the red kidney and the haricot beans, place in a saucepan, cover with cold water, and bring to the boil. Do not add salt. Boil for 10 minutes, then turn down the heat, cover, and simmer for one hour. Add the drained aduki beans 30 minutes before the end of the cooking time. When the beans are soft, drain them and place in a large bowl. Make the French dressing by whisking together the oil and vinegar or lemon juice, sugar, mustard, salt and pepper until well combined. Pour over the warm cooked beans. Add the chopped herbs and onion, and toss lightly. Leave the beans to get completely cold and to soak up the flavours of the herbs before serving.

SPICY BEAN AND PEPPER GOULASH

4 oz each dried red kidney and haricot beans (110 g each)
2 tablespoons sunflower oil
1 onion, peeled and chopped
1 clove garlic, crushed
1 large green pepper, deseeded and chopped
2 large red peppers, deseeded and chopped
8 oz mushrooms, wiped and sliced (225 g)
¼ pint tomato juice (150 ml)
1 or 2 dried red chillis
3 teaspoons paprika
½ teaspoon cumin
salt and freshly ground black pepper

Soak the beans overnight in plenty of cold water, then drain and boil separately in fresh unsalted water until soft. Make sure you cook the red kidney beans correctly, boiling hard for at least ten minutes, and then continuing to cook at a fairly high heat for 1½–2 hours or until tender. Soften the onion and garlic in the oil, then add the peppers and let them cook for a few minutes until soft but not browned. Stir in all the other ingredients, including the drained cooked beans, cover, and simmer gently for half an hour. Serve with rice or pasta.

VEGETARIAN CASSOULET

This is one of those vegetarian dishes that are actually so full of good and interesting things that confirmed meat-eaters don't notice that they are eating a meatless meal.

2 oz each dried haricot beans, butter beans, aduki beans and red kidney beans (55 g)
2 tablespoons corn or sunflower oil
1 small onion, peeled and finely chopped
1 clove garlic, crushed
3 sticks celery, scrubbed and finely chopped
2 or 3 carrots, scrubbed and sliced
4 oz breadcrumbs (110 g)
2 oz farmhouse Cheddar, grated (55 g)
1 tablespoon mixed fresh herbs, chopped, or 1 teaspoon mixed dried herbs
salt and freshly ground black pepper

Put the beans to soak separately overnight. Next day, rinse and drain the kidney beans, cover with plenty of fresh unsalted water, and boil hard for ten minutes. Then add the drained butter beans, add more water if necessary and cook on a fast simmer for half an hour.

Drain and rinse the other beans, add them to the saucepan and continue cooking for about 50 minutes or until all the beans are soft. When cooked, drain all the beans, reserving the liquid. Towards the end of the cooking time, heat the oil in a frying pan and soften the onion and garlic, then add the carrots and celery and allow to cook for ten minutes or so. Add a little of the liquid in which the beans were cooked, and cook the vegetables until just tender.

Now layer the beans and vegetables in an ovenproof dish, starting and finishing with a layer of beans and sprinkling with salt, pepper and herbs as you go. Add three or four more tablespoons of the bean cooking liquor to the casserole, then mix the breadcrumbs and cheese together and sprinkle over the top. Bake, uncovered, for 30–40 minutes at Gas 4, 350 deg F, 180 deg C.
Serves 6.

VEGETARIAN CHILLI

8 oz dried red kidney beans (225 g)
2 tablespoons oil
1 onion, peeled and chopped
1 teaspoon each ground coriander and cumin
4 oz green lentils (225 g)
4 oz red lentils (225 g)
1 clove garlic, crushed
2 small leeks, washed and chopped
2 carrots, scrubbed and chopped
14 oz tin tomatoes and their juice (400 g)
2 teaspoons Tabasco
2 dried chillis

Soak the kidney beans overnight in cold water. Next day, drain them and boil hard for 10 minutes in plenty of fresh unsalted water, then turn the heat down to a fast simmer. In another pan, heat the oil, soften the onion, then stir in the coriander and cumin. Cook for one minute, then add the rest of the ingredients. Add about $\frac{1}{2}$ pint (300 ml) hot water. Cook for 30–40 minutes or until the lentils are soft. Keep them warm until the red beans are soft, then drain the red beans, reserving their liquid, and combine the contents of both pans in a large ovenproof casserole. If the dish looks dry, add some of the reserved bean liquor. Stir well. Cover and cook for 45 minutes at Gas 4, 350 deg F, 180 deg C.
Serves 6.

VEGETARIAN COTTAGE PIE

1 oz butter (25 g)
1 onion, peeled and chopped
1 clove garlic, crushed
1 red pepper, deseeded and chopped
1 pint vegetable stock (600 ml)
2 teaspoons Marmite
8 oz mixed nuts, roughly chopped (225 g)
4 oz fresh breadcrumbs (110 g)
1 tablespoon fresh herbs, chopped
salt and freshly ground black pepper
$1\frac{1}{2}$ lb potatoes, peeled (700 g)
a little milk

Heat the butter and gently sauté the onion, garlic and red pepper. Heat the stock and Marmite together, then mix it with the onion, nuts, red pepper, garlic, breadcrumbs, herbs, and some salt and pepper. Place in an ovenproof dish, cover and bake for 30 minutes at Gas 4, 350 deg F, 180 deg C. Meanwhile, boil the potatoes until soft, drain them, and mash with a little milk. Take the dish from the oven, spoon off some of the liquid if it looks too runny, and cover with the mashed potato. Return to the oven and cook for 20–30 minutes at Gas 6, 400 deg F, 200 deg C.
Serves 4–6.

PASTA DISHES

MACARONI CARBONARA

12 oz macaroni (350 g)
2 oz butter (55 g)
2 tablespoons olive oil
1 small onion, peeled and finely chopped
1 clove garlic, crushed
6 oz streaky bacon, cut into strips (165 g)
4 tablespoons single cream
4 tablespoons Parmesan cheese, grated
3 fresh egg yolks
freshly ground black pepper

to serve:
extra Parmesan cheese, grated

Cook the macaroni for about 12 minutes in lightly salted boiling water until cooked but still firm. Meanwhile, heat the olive oil and butter together, then gently soften the onion and garlic. Add the bacon and fry gently. Beat the cream, egg yolks and Parmesan cheese together. Drain the macaroni, return to the pan, and, off the heat, pour the cream and egg mixture over, and toss well. Do not put the pan back on the heat or the sauce will curdle; the heat of the pan and the macaroni is sufficient to cook the sauce. Stir in the bacon and onion mixture and add black pepper. Serve at once with extra Parmesan cheese sprinkled on top.

PASTA NICOISE

2 tablespoons olive oil
1 large onion, peeled and finely chopped
1 clove garlic, crushed
1 medium red or green pepper, deseeded and chopped
14 oz tin Italian tomatoes (400 g)
1 teaspoon each fresh oregano and basil, finely chopped
salt and freshly ground black pepper
12 oz pasta shells (350 g)
7 oz tin tuna in brine (200 g)
2 tablespoons stoned black olives

Heat the oil in a large frying pan and gently cook the onion and garlic until softened. Add the pepper and continue cooking for five minutes, then add the tomatoes and their juices, herbs and some salt and pepper. Cook for ten minutes, breaking up the tomatoes, until you have a nice, thick sauce. Do not cook on too high a heat, or it will go brown. While this is cooking, cook the pasta in lightly salted boiling water and when it is just tender, drain it and stir it into the tomato sauce together with the flaked tuna fish and the olives. Cook for a couple of minutes more and serve hot, sprinkled with a little cheese and served with crusty bread.
Serves 4–6.

PASTA WITH ASPARAGUS

1 lb pasta shells or bows (450 g)
1 bunch asparagus, washed and trimmed
grated zest of a lemon
2 oz butter (55 g)
4 oz Parma ham, or similar, thinly sliced (110 g)
2 tablespoons double cream
1 tablespoon fresh parsley and chives, finely chopped
¼ teaspoon freshly grated nutmeg
salt and freshly ground black pepper

Put the pasta on to boil in plenty of salted boiling water. Cut the top two or three tender inches off the asparagus stalks, and together with the butter and lemon zest, wrap loosely in foil and place in a steamer or in a colander over a pan of boiling water. Steam the asparagus tips while you prepare the pasta. When the pasta is nearly cooked, chop the remaining asparagus stalks finely and add to the water. Allow to cook until tender, then drain. Stir in the cream, ham, herbs, nutmeg, a little salt and plenty of pepper. Warm through very gently, then divide among four warmed plates or bowls. Unwrap the foil parcel of asparagus tips and use to garnish the pasta, pouring the lemony, buttery juices from the foil over the top of each dish.

PASTA WITH MUSHROOMS

1 oz butter (25 g)
1 tablespoon olive oil
1 small onion, peeled and finely chopped
1 fat clove garlic, crushed
8 oz mushrooms, wiped and sliced (225 g)
1 tablespoon fresh tarragon, chopped
8 oz pasta shapes or tagliatelle (225 g)
2 oz Parmesan cheese, grated (55 g)
salt and freshly ground black pepper

Melt half the butter and the olive oil in a frying pan and gently cook the garlic and onion until soft. Now stir in the mushrooms, tarragon, salt and plenty of black pepper. Add the rest of the butter and allow the mushrooms to soak it up. Meanwhile, put the pasta on to cook in lightly salted boiling water. When just cooked, strain the pasta, and stir in the mushrooms, onion, garlic, and any pan juices. Sprinkle the cheese over the top and serve at once.
Serves 2.

PASTA WITH PORK AND PEAS

2 tablespoons corn or sunflower oil
1 clove garlic, crushed
1 onion, peeled and chopped
1 lb lean pork, finely minced (450 g)
14 oz tin tomatoes (400 g)
2 tablespoons tomato purée
salt and freshly ground black pepper
12 oz pasta shells or spirals (350 g)
4 oz mushrooms, wiped and sliced (110 g)
8 oz frozen peas (225 g)
generous dash of Worcester sauce
2 tablespoons fresh parsley, chopped

Start by heating the oil and gently frying the onion and garlic. When they begin to soften, turn up the heat and fry the pork for about five minutes, until it changes colour. Now add the tomatoes and their juice, the tomato purée, and some salt and pepper. Bring to the boil, then turn down the heat, cover with a lid and simmer for ten minutes or so. Meanwhile, put the pasta on to cook in plenty of lightly salted boiling water. Five minutes before the pasta is ready, add the mushrooms, peas, Worcester sauce and parsley to the meat. Stir well and cook, uncovered, until the peas are cooked through and the sauce has thickened. Serve with the pasta.

RIGATONI WITH CHICKEN LIVERS

1 tablespoon corn or sunflower oil
1 onion, peeled and chopped
1 clove garlic, crushed and chopped
2 slices smoked streaky bacon, chopped
8 oz chicken livers, rinsed and chopped (225 g)
14 oz tin Italian tomatoes (400 g)
salt and freshly ground black pepper
1 tablespoon fresh parsley, chopped
12 oz rigatoni pasta shapes (350 g)

Heat the oil in a frying pan and soften the onion and garlic. Add the bacon and chicken livers, and cook for five minutes more, stirring the livers around until they are brown. Now stir in the tomatoes, parsley, and salt and pepper. You may not need all the juice from the tin of tomatoes; so keep it in reserve until you see how your sauce is thickening up, only adding extra juice if you need to. Meanwhile, cook the pasta according to the instructions on the packet. Drain well, and serve with the sauce with crusty bread and a green salad.

TAGLIATELLE TURKEY

12 oz tagliatelle (350 g)
2 tablespoons sunflower oil
1 small onion, peeled and finely chopped
1 clove garlic, crushed
4 oz mushrooms, wiped and sliced (110 g)
1 oz butter (25 g)
1 tablespoon plain flour
$\frac{1}{4}$ pint dry white wine (150 ml)
$\frac{1}{2}$ pint turkey stock (300 ml)
6 oz cooked turkey meat, cubed (175 g)
4 oz ham, sliced (110 g)
1 tablespoon fresh parsley, chopped
$\frac{1}{4}$ pint single cream (150 ml) (optional)
1 tablespoon olive oil
salt and freshly ground black pepper

Start by putting the pasta to cook in lightly salted boiling water. While it is cooking, heat the oil and soften the onion and garlic, add the mushrooms and cook for a few more minutes. In another pan, melt the butter, add the flour, then gradually stir in the stock and wine. Cook for a few minutes, stirring all the time. Add the onions, garlic, mushrooms, turkey, ham, parsley, and some salt and freshly ground black pepper to the sauce. Stir in the cream, if using, and heat through gently. When the pasta is cooked, drain, toss in olive oil and sprinkle liberally with black pepper, and serve on hot plates with the turkey sauce.
Serves 4–6.

VEGETABLE TAGLIATELLE

2 oz butter (55 g)
1 clove garlic, crushed
1 red onion, peeled and finely chopped
$\frac{1}{2}$ a green pepper, deseeded and chopped
4 oz fresh peas (shelled weight) (110 g)
4 oz French beans, cut into $\frac{1}{2}$ inch (1 cm) pieces (110 g)
2 courgettes, sliced
$1\frac{1}{2}$ oz plain flour (40 g)
$\frac{3}{4}$ pint milk (450 ml)
4 oz farmhouse Cheddar, grated (110 g)
salt and freshly ground black pepper
freshly grated nutmeg
12 oz tagliatelle (350 g)

In a large pan, melt the butter and soften the onion and garlic. Add the green pepper and cook for a few more minutes. Then add the rest of the vegetables and cover. Leave them to cook gently until tender—this will take about 10 minutes. Put the tagliatelle on to cook in some lightly salted boiling water. When the vegetables are cooked, strain them and reserve the buttery juices. Strain the cooked pasta and gently mix it with the vegetables in a large serving dish. Pop in a warm oven to keep warm while you quickly make the sauce with the buttery juices from the vegetables. Put the juices in a pan with the flour and stir well over a low heat until you have a thick paste. Cook for a couple of minutes. Add the milk little by little, stirring all the time. Add seasoning, nutmeg and cheese, and cook for a few minutes more. Pour over the pasta and vegetables, and pop under the grill until lightly browned and bubbling.

RICE DISHES

BAKED RICE PILAFF

This is a tremendous dish for people like me who are usually doing six other things as well as cooking, because the whole lot goes into the oven, cooks itself, and then comes out ready to eat. No panicking over rice boiling over on the hob, or sticking to the pan, or becoming a gluey mess!

4 oz long grain rice (110 g)
2 oz ready-to-eat dried apricots (55 g)
2 oz frozen peas (55 g)
1 oz almonds, flaked (25 g)

2 oz raisins (55 g)
$\frac{1}{2}$ teaspoon salt
$\frac{1}{2}$ teaspoon turmeric
$\frac{3}{4}$ pint boiling water (450 ml)

Mix all the ingredients together in an ovenproof casserole, then cover and cook in the oven for 45 minutes at Gas 4, 350 deg F, 180 deg C, or until the rice is cooked and the liquid absorbed. Check the seasoning before serving. This dish may be eaten hot or cold, on its own or to accompany meat or fish dishes. (It may also be cooked at a very low heat on the hob, but you must stir occasionally to prevent sticking.)

BROWN RICE PILAFF

8 oz long grain brown rice (225 g)
1 pint water (600 ml)
1 level teaspoon salt
$\frac{1}{2}$ teaspoon turmeric
2 tablespoons sunflower oil
1 red onion, peeled and chopped
1 clove garlic, crushed
8 oz frozen peas, or 2 small courgettes, chopped, or 8 oz young carrots, chopped, or a combination (225 g)

1 red pepper, deseeded and chopped
1 green pepper, deseeded and chopped
1 clove garlic, crushed
1 teaspoon garam masala
6 spring onions, chopped
2 oz seedless raisins (55 g)
2 oz flaked almonds, toasted (55 g)

Put the rice into a large saucepan and add the water, salt and turmeric. Bring to the boil, stirring now and then, then turn down the heat to low. Cover tightly and leave to cook very gently, without disturbing the rice, for 45 minutes. Heat the oil in a frying pan, add the chopped red onion, garlic and peppers, together with the courgettes, if using, and soften gently. Simmer the peas and/or carrots in lightly salted boiling water until just tender. Just before the rice is ready, stir the garam masala into the frying pan and cook gently for two minutes. Drain the rice and the peas and/or carrots, and mix lightly together. Mix in the contents of the frying pan. Lightly fork in the chopped spring onions and raisins, and sprinkle with the toasted flaked almonds. Serve hot.
Serves 6.

GREEN RISOTTO

As long as you like rice, risottos make wonderful meals. You can fill them with all sorts of goodies, or leftovers from the fridge, and devise your own favourite combinations.

1 lb courgettes, broccoli or calabrese (450 g)
3 pints chicken or vegetable stock (1.6 litres)
2 tablespoons olive oil
1 onion, peeled and finely chopped
1 clove garlic, crushed
10 oz Italian short grain risotto rice (275 g)
salt and freshly ground black pepper

to serve:
Parmesan cheese, freshly grated

Chop the courgettes, broccoli or calabrese into pieces about one inch (2.5 cm) long and cook in the chicken or vegetable stock for five minutes. Meanwhile, heat the oil in a large frying pan and soften the onion and garlic; add the rice and stir around well until glistening. Remove the vegetables from the stock with a slotted spoon and add to the frying pan. Stir well, then add about a third of the stock. Season. Simmer until the stock is absorbed, then add more stock little by little, until the rice is cooked. You may not need all the stock. Check the seasoning. Serve immediately, liberally sprinkled with Parmesan cheese.

HAM, CHICKEN AND MUSHROOM RISOTTO

2 tablespoons olive oil
1 oz butter (25 g)
1 large onion, peeled and chopped
1 stick celery, scrubbed and chopped
8 oz mushrooms, wiped and sliced (225 g)
1 clove garlic, crushed
8 oz short grain risotto rice (225 g)
1 pint chicken stock (600 ml)
4 oz cold cooked chicken, cubed (110 g)
4 oz ham, chopped (110 g)
salt and freshly ground black pepper
1 tablespoon fresh parsley, chopped
1 tablespoon Parmesan cheese, freshly grated

Heat the oil and butter in a large frying pan and fry the onion gently until softened. Add the celery, mushrooms and garlic to the pan and cook for a few more minutes, stirring well. Add the rice and continue to stir fry for a minute or two. Now add the stock and some seasoning, bring to the boil, then turn down to a gentle simmer. Stir in the chicken and ham, and simmer gently until the rice has absorbed all the liquid and is cooked through. Stir in the parsley just before serving, and sprinkle with the freshly grated Parmesan cheese.

KEDGEREE

1 lb undyed smoked haddock fillets (450 g)
½ pint milk (275 ml)
½ pint water (275 ml)
2 oz butter (55 g)
1 large onion, peeled and chopped
½ teaspoon hot curry powder
8 oz brown rice (225 g)
2 hard boiled eggs, chopped
2 heaped tablespoons fresh parsley, chopped
salt and freshly ground black pepper

Poach the haddock in the milk and water until tender. Strain, reserving the poaching liquid. Melt the butter in a frying pan and soften the onion for about five minutes, then stir in the curry powder and cook for a couple of minutes, stirring well. Add the rice, all the fish liquid, and a little salt and pepper. Cover and simmer gently until the rice is cooked and all the liquid absorbed. Flake the haddock, mix it with the eggs, stir in the rice and onions, and lastly mix in the chopped parsley. Serve for breakfast, brunch, or lunch.

RICE AND LENTIL BAKE

1 tablespoon sunflower oil
1 onion, peeled and chopped
1 clove garlic, crushed
1 stick celery, washed and chopped
4 oz red lentils (110 g)
4 oz brown rice (110 g)
1 pint chicken or vegetable stock (600 ml)
1 bay leaf, crushed
1 sprig thyme
6 tomatoes, roughly chopped
2 oz walnuts, chopped (55 g)
salt and freshly ground black pepper

for the topping:
2 oz farmhouse Cheddar, grated (55 g)
2 oz fresh brown breadcrumbs (55 g)
1 oz sesame seeds (25 g)

In a large frying pan, heat the oil, then add the onions, garlic and celery. Cook gently until softened. Add the rice and red lentils and stir them around to get them coated in oil. Now add about two thirds of the stock, the herbs and the tomatoes. Cover with a lid and cook gently for 25–30 minutes, stirring occasionally and adding the rest of the stock if needed. When the rice and lentils are cooked, they should have absorbed all the liquid. Remove the bay leaf, thyme, and any obvious tomato skins. Stir in the walnuts and season with salt and pepper. Place in a deep ovenproof serving dish, mix the topping ingredients together, sprinkle over the rice and lentils, and place in the oven at Gas 6, 400 deg F, 200 deg C, for 10 -15 minutes. Serves 4–6.

RICE, BEAN SPROUT AND SWEETCORN SALAD

8 oz long grain brown rice (225 g)
8 oz fresh bean sprouts (225 g)
1 green pepper
1 small tin sweetcorn

for the dressing:
4 tablespoons olive oil
juice of $\frac{1}{2}$ a lemon
$\frac{1}{2}$ teaspoon sugar
$\frac{1}{2}$ teaspoon English mustard powder
salt and freshly ground black pepper

Cook the rice in a large pan of lightly salted boiling water until just tender. Drain and rinse with hot water. Meanwhile, wash and drain the bean sprouts; deseed and chop the green pepper; and drain the canned sweetcorn. Whisk the dressing ingredients together, or shake them up in a screw topped jar. Mix the rice with the bean sprouts, sweetcorn and pepper, then add the dressing and toss well. Cover and chill for two hours before serving.
Serves 6 as a side salad.

RICE WITH PISTACHIO NUTS

8 oz Basmati rice (225 g)
1 tablespoon sunflower oil
1 onion, peeled and finely chopped
1 pint boiling water (600 ml)
salt and freshly ground black pepper
4 oz pistachio nuts, shelled (110 g)

Start by rinsing the rice in several changes of cold water; I find this easiest to do by placing the rice in a sieve and shaking it around under the cold running tap. When the water runs clear, the rice is ready for cooking. Now heat the oil in a large saucepan and gently soften the onion. Add the rice, boiling water and some salt and pepper, cover, and simmer gently for ten minutes. Toast the nuts under the grill for a few minutes. Test to see if the rice has absorbed all the water and is cooked; if not, simmer for a few more minutes. Take off the heat and fluff up with a fork, lightly stir in the toasted pistachios and serve hot. If you need to keep the rice warm while serving a first course, dot it with butter and cover with foil or greaseproof paper and keep warm in the oven.

VEGETABLES

Broccoli · Courgettes · Potatoes · Runner beans · Spinach · peas.

VEGETABLES

The English are famed for their culinary abuse of vegetables. (And I don't mean British, either—the Scots do interesting things with turnips and swedes, and the Welsh are well known for the things they can do with leeks.)

Our neglect of vegetables may date back to Victorian times, when tables groaned with three times as much meat as we would consider reasonable now, or go back to times when even poor country folk would have their pig to furnish them with a year's meat, with vegetables accorded a very poor second place.

I was lucky as a child, in that my father was an enterprising kitchen gardener. I must have been one of the first children in Somerset to eat courgettes, aubergines and peppers. But it wasn't until I went to France as a teenager that I discovered that tomatoes had flavour, that courgettes could make a meal on their own, and that haricot beans, tossed in olive oil and black pepper, could also be served as a course in their own right.

Now, thanks both to foreign travel and the vegetarian lobby, we treat our vegetables with more respect. No decent restaurant or self-respecting hostess would dare serve soggy Brussels sprouts, stringy runner beans, or frozen peas. As I hope this section shows, many vegetable dishes deserve to be served as a course in their own right; and all vegetables, however humble, deserve better treatment than 20 minutes hard boiling in heavily salted water.

Broccoli with almonds
Chinese leaf stir fry
Colcannon (traditional Irish cabbage and potatoes)
Courgettes Provençale
Flaky mushroom and walnut pie
French peas
Green beans in tomato sauce
Greek leeks
Grilled summer vegetables
Hot new potato salad
Kohl rabi with cheese
Potato gratin dauphinois

Root vegetables au gratin
Runner bean stir fry
Special cauliflower cheese
Spicy cauliflower
Spicy marrow crumble
Spinach and yogurt pie
Spinach tart
Spring greens stir fry
Stuffed red cabbage
Tomato soufflé
Vegetarian bake
Vegetable hotpot
Watercress and mushroom roulade

BROCCOLI WITH ALMONDS

$1\frac{1}{2}$ lb broccoli, washed and trimmed (700 g)
2 oz butter (55 g)
2 oz flaked almonds (55 g)
juice and grated zest of $\frac{1}{2}$ a lemon
salt and freshly ground black pepper

Cook the broccoli in lightly salted boiling water until just tender. This will take 10–15 minutes. Drain well and transfer to a warmed serving dish, and keep warm. When the broccoli is nearly cooked, melt the butter in a small saucepan, and add the almonds and lemon zest. Fry over a gentle heat, turning the almonds over now and then, until golden brown. Stir in the lemon juice, season with black pepper and salt if needed, and pour over the broccoli. This dish goes very well with fish or chicken.

CHINESE LEAF STIR FRY

1 head Chinese leaf cabbage
1 tablespoon sesame seed oil
1 clove garlic, crushed
1 inch piece root ginger, peeled and crushed (2.5 cm)
2 tablespoons rich soy sauce
1 dried chilli
1 tablespoon sweet sherry
2 teaspoons brown sugar
$\frac{1}{2}$ teaspoon ground coriander
6 spring onions, chopped
1 tablespoon sesame seeds, toasted
freshly ground black pepper

Trim and wash the Chinese leaf cabbage and cut into 1 inch (2.5 cm) shreds. Heat the sesame oil in a wok or large frying pan, then add the garlic and ginger. Cook for a minute, stirring well, then add the soy sauce, chilli, sherry, sugar and coriander. Stir well and cook for another couple of minutes, making sure that the sugar dissolves. Turn up the heat and add the Chinese leaves and spring onions. Stir fry them over a high heat for about five minutes, until the leaves are well coated in the spicy sauce and start to collapse. If the leaves look as though they might stick to the bottom of the pan, add a little hot water. Stir in the sesame seeds and add some black pepper just before serving. Do not overcook the leaves, there is nothing worse than a soggy stir fry!

COLCANNON
A traditional Irish cabbage and potato dish

12 oz cabbage, trimmed, washed and finely shredded (350 g)
8 oz potatoes, peeled weight (225 g)
1 fat leek, white only, washed and chopped
½ pint milk or single cream (300 ml)
salt and freshly ground black pepper
freshly grated nutmeg
1 oz butter (25 g)

Cook the cabbage in plenty of lightly salted boiling water and drain well. In another pan, cook the potatoes and when they are soft, mash well. In a third pan, cook the leek in the milk or cream, simmering very gently until tender. Drain the leek, reserving the juice. Mix the leek, cabbage and potato together, and add enough of the milk or cream from cooking the leek to make a soft, but not sloppy consistency. Add salt, pepper and nutmeg to taste, and pile into a heated serving dish. Keep warm while you melt the butter, then make a well in the centre of the colcannon, pour in the melted butter and serve at once. Serve on its own or with sausages or chops.

COURGETTES PROVENCALE

1 lb young courgettes (450 g)
2 teaspoons salt
3 tablespoons olive oil
2–3 tablespoons plain wholemeal flour
4 oz long grain white rice (110 g)
½ pint chicken stock (300 ml)
1 clove garlic, crushed
1 onion, peeled and thinly sliced
2 ripe tomatoes, peeled and thinly sliced
2 teaspoons fresh thyme leaves
salt and freshly ground black pepper
3 oz farmhouse Cheddar, grated (75 g)

Wipe the courgettes; top and tail them, and cut diagonally into thin, oval slices. Put them in a colander and sprinkle with the salt. Leave them for about 15 minutes, then rinse under the cold tap and pat dry on kitchen paper. Sprinkle with the flour and fry in hot oil in batches in a large frying pan until browned on both sides. Keep the cooked courgettes warm in a bowl lined with kitchen paper. Put the rice on to cook in the chicken stock while the courgettes are frying. When all the courgettes are cooked, gently soften the onion and garlic in the same frying pan, and then add the tomatoes. When the rice is cooked, drain it and spoon it into the base of a greased, shallow ovenproof dish. Layer half the courgettes on top. Sprinkle in half the thyme and some salt and pepper. Add the onions, garlic and tomatoes, sprinkle on the rest of the thyme, more seasoning, and then layer on the rest of the courgettes. Sprinkle the cheese on top and bake for 10 minutes at Gas 6, 400 deg F, 200 deg C and then quickly brown under a hot grill.

FLAKY MUSHROOM AND WALNUT PIE

3 oz butter (75 g)
1 large onion, peeled and chopped
2 cloves garlic, crushed
1 lb mushrooms, wiped and chopped (450 g)
3 oz walnuts, chopped (75 g)
2 tablespoons fresh parsley, chopped, and 1 tablespoon fresh sage, chopped, or 2 teaspoons mixed dried herbs
4 oz wholewheat breadcrumbs (110 g)
1 egg, beaten
salt and freshly ground black pepper
14 oz filo pastry, thawed (400 g)
1 tablespoon sesame seeds

Heat half the butter in a large frying pan, and add the onion and garlic and fry gently until softened. Add the mushrooms, turn the heat up a little, and fry for another five minutes. Remove from the heat, then mix in the walnuts, parsley and sage, breadcrumbs, the egg, and plenty of salt and black pepper. Melt the remaining butter in a small pan and use a little to grease a 13 × 9 inch (33 × 23 cm) Swiss roll tin. Line the tin with half the filo leaves, brushing melted butter on to each layer of pastry as you put it on. Spread the mushroom and walnut mixture over the pastry, then cover with the remaining filo leaves, brushing them with the remaining butter. Score the top layers of pastry with a very sharp knife to form a pattern of diamonds, brush with melted butter and sprinkle with sesame seeds. Cook in a preheated oven at Gas 5, 375 deg F, 190 deg C, for 25 minutes, and serve hot, cut into slices, with a crunchy green salad or a selection of hot vegetables.

FRENCH PEAS

1½ lb fresh or frozen shelled peas (700 g)
1 lettuce, washed and shredded
12 baby onions or shallots
6 stalks of fresh parsley
2 oz butter (55 g)
1 teaspoon salt
2 teaspoons sugar

to garnish:
1 tablespoon fresh parsley, finely chopped

Put all the ingredients into a saucepan with five or six tablespoons of water, bring to the boil, then turn down the heat immediately and simmer, covered, for 30–40 minutes. This is the cooking time for fresh peas; frozen ones will take less time, but check to see that the onions are cooked. Remove the parsley stalks and sprinkle with fresh parsley before serving. Serve piping hot.
Serves 4–6.

GREEN BEANS IN TOMATO SAUCE

1 lb ripe tomatoes (450 g)
1½ lb French beans (700 g)
2 tablespoons olive oil
1 small onion, peeled and finely chopped
1 clove garlic, crushed
salt and freshly ground black pepper
1 tablespoon each fresh parsley and basil, chopped

Skin the tomatoes by plunging them into boiling water for a few minutes; remove them and when cool enough to handle, peel away the skins. Chop them roughly. Top, tail and halve the French beans, then cook in boiling salted water for just three minutes. Drain well. Heat the oil in a saucepan, add the onion and fry gently until just beginning to colour. Stir in the chopped tomatoes and crushed garlic. Cook, covered, for about five minutes. Mix in the beans, cover, and cook for another 10–15 minutes, or until the beans are tender and the sauce has reduced slightly. Stir in the herbs and seasoning just before serving.
Serves 6.

GREEK LEEKS

1 lb young fresh leeks (450 g)
6 parsley stalks
1 bay leaf, crushed
1 sprig thyme
6 peppercorns, roughly crushed
6 coriander seeds, roughly crushed
2 tablespoons olive oil
2 tablespoons lemon juice
¾ pint water (425 ml)
¼ teaspoon salt
1 small onion, peeled and roughly chopped
1 inner celery stalk, scrubbed and roughly chopped

Place all the ingredients except the leeks in a large saucepan and bring to the boil. Turn down the heat and simmer gently for ten minutes. Meanwhile, trim and wash the leeks, discarding most of the green part. Slice into two inch (5 cm) lengths. Add the leeks to the simmering vegetable stock and cook for another 10–15 minutes, or until the leeks are tender. If serving hot, remove the leeks to a hot serving dish, strain the stock, discard herbs, celery, etc, and return the stock to the pan. Boil hard until it is reduced enough just to give the leeks a good coating. Pour over the leeks and serve. If serving cold, leave the leeks to get cold in the stock, then remove them with a draining spoon and serve garnished with a few Greek olives.
Serves 4–6.

GRILLED SUMMER VEGETABLES

2–3 cloves garlic, peeled and crushed
1 teaspoon salt
2 tablespoons fresh basil, chopped
2 tablespoons fresh parsley, chopped
$\frac{1}{4}$–$\frac{1}{2}$ pint olive oil (150–300 ml)
1 medium aubergine
2–3 small courgettes
4 oz mushrooms, wiped (110 g)
1 red pepper, deseeded
1 green pepper, deseeded

Mash the garlic and salt together with the flat blade of a knife or in a pestle and mortar, then mix in the herbs and $\frac{1}{4}$ pint (150 ml) of the olive oil. Chop the vegetables into bite-sized pieces and toss them all in the oil, adding more oil if needed to get them well-coated. Leave in the fridge for 4–8 hours. When ready to cook, spread the vegetables over a grill pan, drizzle on any remaining oil, and grill for 10–15 minutes, shaking around or turning occasionally. The vegetables should be soft and slightly charred. Serve at once. This dish is excellent with roast or grilled chicken, and is also good with barbecued dishes.

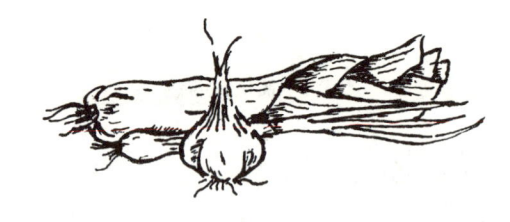

HOT NEW POTATO SALAD

$1\frac{1}{2}$ lb new potatoes, washed (700 g)
$\frac{1}{2}$ oz butter (15 g)
6 spring onions, trimmed and chopped
5 fl oz soured cream (140 ml)
salt and freshly ground black pepper
3–4 sprigs of fresh tarragon or 3–4 fronds of fresh dill

Start by putting the potatoes to cook in their skins in some lightly salted boiling water. While they are cooking, melt the butter, add the spring onions, and cook them very gently for about five minutes. Stir in the soured cream, some salt and pepper, and the tarragon or dill (dill is lovely if you are serving this salad with fish, tarragon goes well with chicken or pork.) Heat through gently; do not allow to boil. Drain the potatoes and place in a warmed serving dish. Pour the herby sauce over them and serve at once.

KOHL RABI WITH CHEESE

1 lb kohl rabi, scrubbed or peeled and sliced very thinly (450 g)
½ pint single cream or milk (275 ml)
4 oz Gruyère or Emmental cheese, thinly sliced (110 g)
½ teaspoon freshly grated nutmeg
salt and freshly ground black pepper

Steam or boil the sliced kohl rabi until it is just beginning to go soft. This will take 5–10 minutes. Drain well. Place in a shallow, greased baking dish, with the slices overlapping. Season with salt, pepper and nutmeg. Pour the cream or milk over the top. Arrange the slices of cheese on top, cover with the foil or a lid and bake in the oven for 40 minutes at Gas 4, 350 deg F, 180 deg C. Uncover during the last 15 minutes to allow the cheese to brown. Celeriac and turnips also cook well this way.

POTATO GRATIN DAUPHINOIS

1½ lb waxy potatoes, scrubbed or peeled and sliced ¼ inch (5 mm) thick (700 g)
1 clove garlic, crushed
1½ oz butter (40 g)
salt and freshly ground black pepper
¼ teaspoon freshly grated nutmeg
1 small turnip, scrubbed or peeled and sliced thinly
¾ pint single cream (425 ml)

Pat the prepared potatoes dry or leave them on a clean cloth to soak up some of their excess moisture. Grease a gratin, or shallow ovenproof, dish with the butter and make a layer of half the sliced potatoes. Season with salt, pepper, nutmeg and garlic. Make another layer of turnip, season again, and then finish off with the rest of the potatoes. Season again and then pour on the cream; this should come up to the top level of potatoes but no further. Dot with the remaining butter and bake for 1¼ hours at Gas 4, 350 deg F, 180 deg C, and then turn up the heat to Gas 6, 400 deg F, 200 deg C for 15 minutes, to brown the top layer of potatoes. Serve hot.

ROOT VEGETABLES AU GRATIN

1 potato, scrubbed or peeled
2 carrots, scrubbed or peeled
1 parsnip, scrubbed
2 small turnips, scrubbed
2 tablespoons corn or sunflower oil
3 or 4 sticks celery, scrubbed and chopped
1 onion, peeled and chopped

for the cheese sauce:
1 oz plain flour (25 g)
1½ oz butter (40 g)
1 pint milk (600 ml)
2 oz farmhouse Cheddar, grated (55 g)
1 teaspoon freshly grated nutmeg
salt and freshly ground black pepper

topping:
2 oz fresh brown breadcrumbs (55 g)

Cut the vegetables into bite-sized pieces. Place in a pan of lightly salted boiling water and simmer gently until just tender. Heat the oil in a frying pan and then soften the onion and celery. In another small pan, melt the butter and, over a gentle heat, stir in the flour until it forms a smooth paste. Add the milk little by little until you have a smooth sauce. Add the cheese, nutmeg, and some salt and pepper. Cook gently until the cheese melts, then take off the heat at once, or it will go stringy. Drain all the vegetables and arrange them in an ovenproof dish. Pour the cheese sauce over them, and sprinkle with the breadcrumbs. Bake at Gas 4, 350 deg F, 180 deg C for about 20 minutes. This is good on its own as a cheap supper dish, or as an accompaniment to simple meat dishes.

RUNNER BEAN STIR FRY

12 oz runner beans, sliced thinly (350 g)
12 oz bean sprouts (350 g)
8 oz tin water chestnuts, drained and sliced (225 g)
2 tablespoons sunflower oil
1 tablespoon wine vinegar
1 tablespoon red wine
1 tablespoon soy sauce
2 teaspoons sugar
½ teaspoon garlic salt

Start by whisking together the oil, vinegar, wine, soy sauce, sugar and garlic salt. Then bring a large pan of water to the boil and blanch the bean sprouts and the runner beans for one minute. Drain. Heat the oil in a large frying pan or wok, and stir fry the water chestnuts. Remove to a hot plate when they are beginning to brown. Now stir fry the runner beans and bean sprouts in the same pan, keeping the heat up and stirring all the time. After two minutes, replace the water chestnuts, and stir in the whisked sauce. Stir fry for one minute, then serve immediately.

SPECIAL CAULIFLOWER CHEESE

1 large cauliflower, washed and divided into florets
4 hard-boiled eggs, shelled and halved
4 oz lean ham, roughly chopped (110 g)
1 oz butter (25 g)
1 oz plain flour, sifted (25 g)
½ pint milk (300 ml)
3 oz farmhouse Cheddar, grated (75 g)
salt and freshly ground black pepper
2 tablespoons double cream (optional)

Boil or steam the cauliflower until just cooked but not too soft. Meanwhile, make the cheese sauce. Melt the butter, stir in the flour and cook for one minute, stirring all the time. Add the milk little by little until you have a smooth sauce, then stir in the cheese and some salt and pepper. Allow the cheese to melt, then take off the heat. Stir in the cream, if using. Arrange the ham in the base of a greased ovenproof dish. Arrange the cooked and drained cauliflower on top with the eggs, then pour the sauce over the top. Bake in the oven for 15–20 minutes at Gas 4, 350 deg F, 180 deg C.

SPICY CAULIFLOWER

2 tablespoons oil
2 onions, peeled and chopped
½ a green pepper, deseeded and chopped
2 teaspoons turmeric
2 teaspoons ground cumin
1 teaspoon ground coriander
8 oz green lentils (225 g)
1 pint vegetable stock (600 ml)
juice and grated zest of ½ a lemon
1 teaspoon Tabasco
1 cauliflower, washed and divided into florets
2 oz walnuts, chopped (55 g)
salt and freshly ground black pepper

Heat the oil, then gently soften the onions and green pepper. Stir in the turmeric, cumin and coriander and fry for one minute. Add the lentils and stir well. Add the stock, lemon juice and zest and Tabasco. Bring to the boil, turn down the heat, cover and simmer for 20–30 minutes until the lentils are nearly cooked. (The cooking time will depend on the age of the lentils; the older they are, the longer they will take.) Now add the cauliflower, stir, cover and cook until tender. This will take 10–15 minutes, and you may need to add some more stock or water. Stir in the nuts, season, and serve hot. Serve with garlic bread and a green salad.

SPICY MARROW CRUMBLE

If you have a gardener in the family, you will be familiar with the problem of what to do with the autumn's oversized marrows. This solution is really rather good and I certainly prefer it to the predictable stuffed marrow.

1 oz butter (25 g)
1 tablespoon corn or sunflower oil
1 onion, peeled and chopped
1 clove garlic, crushed
½ teaspoon each ground cumin and freshly grated nutmeg
1 teaspoon crushed coriander seeds
1 lb marrow or large courgettes (deseeded and peeled weight) cut into chunks (450 g)
2 tomatoes, skinned and chopped
1 oz wholemeal flour (25 g)
¼ pint milk (150 ml)
½ pint vegetable stock (300 ml)
2 oz hazelnuts or walnuts, roughly chopped (55 g)
salt and freshly ground black pepper

for the topping:
4 oz margarine (110 g)
6 oz wholemeal flour (175 g)
4 oz farmhouse Cheddar, grated (110 g)
2 oz sesame seeds (55 g)

Heat the butter and oil together in a large frying pan, then gently soften the onion and garlic. Add the spices, stir around well and cook for a couple of minutes. Now add the marrow and tomatoes and stir well. Cover and cook gently for about 20 minutes, or until the marrow starts to feel tender.

Stir in the flour, cook for one minute, then add the stock and milk little by little, stirring well. Add the nuts, season with salt and pepper, and leave to simmer for another 15–20 minutes.

Meanwhile, make the crumble topping. Rub in the fat and flour, then stir in the cheese and seeds. Spoon the marrow mixture into a large ovenproof dish and sprinkle the crumble mixture over the top. Place in the oven and bake at Gas 5, 375 deg F, 190 deg C for half an hour.
Serves 4–6.

SPINACH AND YOGURT PIE

2 lb spinach, washed and trimmed (1 kg)
1 oz butter (25 g)
8 oz streaky bacon, chopped (225 g)
1 large onion, peeled and chopped
10 oz thick natural yogurt (275 g)
2 eggs, beaten
2 oz farmhouse Cheddar, grated (55 g)
salt and freshly ground black pepper
½ teaspoon freshly grated nutmeg
1 tablespoon Parmesan, grated

to garnish:
fresh parsley, chopped

Melt the butter in a large saucepan and cook the spinach until soft; fresh spinach will take 10–15 minutes, but if you use frozen it will take less time. Stir occasionally, and make sure the spinach doesn't stick and burn. Drain, chop finely, and place in a buttered ovenproof shallow dish. While the spinach is cooking, gently fry the bacon until the fat starts to run, then add the onion and cook until the bacon is browned and the onion soft. Spoon on to the spinach. Now beat together the yogurt, eggs, grated Cheddar, nutmeg, and some salt and pepper. Pour over the spinach and bacon and sprinkle the Parmesan on top. Bake in the oven at Gas 5, 375 deg F, 190 deg C, for 25 minutes, until the top is set and lightly browned. Serve hot, with crusty bread.

SPINACH TART

8 oz puff pastry, defrosted if frozen (225 g)
1 lb spinach (450 g)
1½ oz butter (40 g)
salt and freshly ground black pepper
4–6 tinned anchovies, soaked in a little milk
1 hard-boiled egg

Roll out the pastry and use to line an 8 inch (20 cm) flan tin. Blanch the spinach in boiling water for two minutes, then drain and squeeze dry in a clean tea towel. Chop the spinach small, then work in the butter and some salt and pepper. Spread this mixture over the pastry, then arrange the anchovies on top. Use any left over pastry to make pastry leaves, and place on a baking sheet separately. Brush the leaves and the edge of the flan with milk or beaten egg, then bake for 25–35 minutes at Gas 7, 425 deg F, 225 deg C, removing the leaves from the oven when they are risen and browned. When the tart is cooked, chop the hard-boiled egg into rounds, and arrange around the edge of the tart. Decorate the centre with the pastry leaves. Serve hot or warm.

SPRING GREENS STIR FRY

2 tablespoons sesame oil
½ inch piece root ginger, peeled and crushed (1 cm)
2 or 3 young carrots, scrubbed and cut into thin strips
4 oz button mushrooms, wiped and sliced (110 g)
1 small bunch spring greens, washed and shredded
4 oz bean sprouts, rinsed and drained (110 g)
3–4 spring onions, whites only, chopped
1 tablespoon sweet sherry
1 tablespoon soy sauce
salt and freshly ground black pepper

Heat the oil in a wok or large frying pan until very hot. Stir fry the carrots and ginger for one minute in the hot oil, then add the mushrooms. Stir for another minute, then add the cabbage, bean sprouts and spring onions and stir fry for a few more minutes. Sprinkle in the sherry and soy sauce, season with salt and pepper, and serve hot.

STUFFED RED CABBAGE

1 medium red cabbage
3 rashers smoked streaky bacon, chopped
1 onion, peeled and chopped
1 clove garlic, crushed
2 oz red lentils (55 g)
½ pint beef or vegetable stock (275 ml)
2 oz walnuts, chopped (55 g)
1 oz farmhouse Cheddar, grated (25 g)
2 cloves
½ teaspoon ground cinnamon
salt and freshly ground black pepper
1 oz butter (25 g)

Heat the bacon in a frying pan and when the fat begins to run, add the onion and garlic. Allow to sweat for a few minutes, then add the lentils, stir, and add the stock. Put a lid on the pan and simmer gently for 20 -30 minutes or until the lentils are soft. Check from time to time and add more stock or water if needed. Meanwhile, trim the red cabbage and cut out some of the hard stalk. Cut off the top for a "lid", then scoop out the inside leaves to make a large hollow for the stuffing. Shred the inside leaves finely and reserve. When the lentils are ready, stir in the walnuts, cheese, spices, and season. Grease a fairly deep baking dish with a little of the butter, then stuff the cabbage with the lentil and nut mixture. Place a dot of butter on top, then put on the "lid". Place in the baking dish, then arrange the shredded cabbage around it, together with any leftover stuffing mixture, and dot with the rest of the butter. Cover and bake at Gas 4, 350 deg F, 180 deg C for 1½–2 hours or until you can pierce the cabbage shell with a sharp knife.

TOMATO SOUFFLE

1½ lb ripe tomatoes (700 g)
1¾ oz butter (45 g)
1 tablespoon fresh basil, chopped
1 tablespoon plain flour
¼ pint milk (150 ml)
salt and freshly ground black pepper
¼ teaspoon freshly grated nutmeg
1 tablespoon tomato purée
4 fresh eggs, separated
1 oz Parmesan cheese, grated (25 g)

Roughly chop the tomatoes and place in a pan with 1 oz (25 g) of the butter, and the basil. Cook gently. Meanwhile, gently melt the remaining butter, stir in the flour, cook for one minute, and then add the milk little by little. Season with salt, pepper and nutmeg. Cook very gently for five minutes, stirring now and then. Take off the heat. Sieve the tomatoes to remove skins and pips, then add to the white sauce. Beat the egg yolks, then add to the sauce together with the tomato purée. Now whisk the egg whites until stiff, then fold gently into the tomato mixture. Transfer to a greased soufflé dish, sprinkle with the cheese, and bake at Gas 7, 425 deg F, 220 deg C, for 20–25 minutes until risen and set. Serve immediately.

VEGETARIAN BAKE

1 lb potatoes, scrubbed and sliced (450 g)
1 large onion, peeled and chopped
2 cloves garlic, crushed
2 medium courgettes, wiped and sliced
2 tablespoons vegetable oil
7 oz can red kidney beans (700 g)
4 tomatoes, chopped (700 g)
2 oz walnuts, chopped (55 g)
1 oz margarine (25 g)
$1\frac{1}{2}$ oz plain wholemeal flour (40 g)
$\frac{1}{2}$ pint milk (300 ml)
4 oz farmhouse Cheddar, grated (110 g)
salt and freshly ground black pepper

Boil the potatoes in lightly salted water for 10 minutes or so, until they are just cooked through but not soft. Meanwhile, fry the onion, garlic and courgettes in the oil until softened but not coloured. Stir in the drained kidney beans, tomatoes and walnuts, and season. Continue cooking for another five minutes. While the vegetables and potatoes are cooking, melt the margarine in a small saucepan and blend in the flour and cook for one minute. Add the milk little by little until you have a smooth sauce. Season. Turn the nut and vegetable mixture into a greased ovenproof gratin or similar shallow dish. Drain the potatoes and arrange the slices on top of the vegetables. Remove the sauce from the heat and stir in the cheese, reserving a little for topping. Beat until the sauce is glossy, then pour over the potatoes and sprinkle the rest of the cheese on top. Bake, uncovered, in the oven at Gas 5, 375 deg F, 190 deg C for 30–40 minutes, until golden brown and bubbly. Serve hot, with a crisp salad and bread.

VEGETABLE HOTPOT

1 tablespoon corn oil
1 clove garlic, crushed
1 onion, peeled
3 carrots, scrubbed
2 bay leaves, crushed
1 teaspoon caraway seeds
1 small parsnip, scrubbed
½ a small swede, scrubbed
4 potatoes, scrubbed
4 oz can black eye beans, drained (125 g)
4 tomatoes, peeled
¾ pint vegetable stock (450 ml)
3 tablespoons red wine
2 teaspoons soy sauce
salt and freshly ground black pepper

Roughly chop all the vegetables into similar sizes. Heat the oil in a large saucepan and gently sauté the onion and garlic until soft. Add the carrots, bay leaves and caraway seeds and stir fry for a few minutes. Add the parsnip, swede and potatoes, and cook for a few more minutes. Add the rest of the ingredients, cover, and simmer gently until the potatoes are soft. Check the seasoning and serve hot.

WATERCRESS AND MUSHROOM ROULADE

Roulades look immensely difficult to make but actually they are quite easy. This one looks lovely and the combination of flavours is very good.

for the roulade:
1 bunch watercress, washed
½ teaspoon garlic salt
4 oz farmhouse Cheddar, grated (110 g)
6 large fresh eggs, separated

for the filling:
2 oz unsalted butter (55 g)
1 lb mushrooms, wiped and sliced (450 g)
2 oz plain flour (55 g)
¼ pint milk (150 ml)
1 tablespoon sherry

Start by greasing a Swiss roll tin and lining it with baking parchment to come one inch (2.5 cm) above the sides. Blanch the watercress for one minute in boiling water, then drain and chop well, discarding any tough stems.

Beat the egg yolks and garlic salt together until creamy. Add the cheese and watercress. Whisk the egg whites until stiff, and stir one spoonful into the yolks to soften the mixture, then carefully fold in the rest of the whites.

Pour into the prepared Swiss roll tin. Bake for 12–15 minutes at Gas 6, 400 deg F, 200 deg C until firm. Turn out on to baking parchment liberally sprinkled with freshly ground pepper.

While the roulade cooks, make the filling. Melt the butter and soften the mushrooms. When they are cooked, remove them with a slotted spoon and whisk the juices with the flour, milk and sherry until you have a nice thick sauce. Add the mushrooms, stir, then spread over the hot roulade. Roll up carefully and serve at once.

SALADS

Fennel · Avocado · Garlic · Carrots · Chinese Leaf · Celery · Mint

SALADS

I love concocting new salads, experimenting with different combinations of flavours, textures and colours. Making different dressings to suit different ingredients is a pleasureable task, too.

Being a rather lazy person, I also like making salads because I have discovered that the quicker they are made, generally the better they are. If you mess around with the ingredients too much, they begin to wilt and fade and look battered.

The exception is real mayonnaise, which is time consuming to prepare. But it is an acquired taste, and since none of my family has acquired it, I don't often make it. Occasionally, however, I will drizzle olive oil into a beaten egg yolk, and then add masses of crushed garlic, and then cut up raw vegetables to dip into it. Afterwards, as I breathe fumes over all and sundry, I wish they shared my passion! Where a mayonnaise is required for the recipes in this section, a good bought one is perfectly adequate.

Beef salad with warm ginger dressing
Carrot salad
Chicken and avocado salad
Chicken and pineapple salad
Chicken liver salad
Chinese leaf salad
Cucumber, yogurt and mint salad
Fennel salad
Feta and watermelon salad
Goat's cheese salad
Hot crab salad
Italian salmon salad
Italian winter salad
Leafy green salad
Orange and peanut coleslaw
Potato, celery and walnut salad
Seafood salad
Tarragon pork salad
Tomato salad
Turkey and apple salad
Waldorf salad
Watercress and mushroom salad

BEEF SALAD WITH WARM GINGER DRESSING

1 lb rump steak in one piece, trimmed of fat (450 g)
3 tablespoons beef stock
1 tablespoon soy sauce
1 tablespoon ground ginger
1 clove garlic, crushed
2 courgettes, wiped
2 carrots, scrubbed
2 oz broad beans, shelled weight (55 g)
4 oz mangetout peas (110 g)
2 inside sticks celery, scrubbed
1 tablespoon olive oil

Lay the steak in a shallow dish. Combine the stock, soy sauce, ginger and garlic, and pour over the beef. Leave to marinate for two hours. With a very sharp paring knife, cut lengthwise grooves into the courgettes and carrots. Slice them thinly. Chop the celery. Place all the vegetables in a bowl. Remove the steak from the marinade and grill for 3–7 minutes on each side, depending on how you like your beef. Meanwhile, put the marinade in a small saucepan and bring to the boil, remove from the heat, and stir in the oil. Pour this dressing over the vegetables and mix well. Transfer the vegetables to a serving dish. Cut the steak into thin slices and arrange on top of the vegetables. Serve at once.

CARROT SALAD

1 lb carrots, scrubbed and grated (450 g)
4 small courgettes, washed and grated
2 oz raisins (55 g)
4 tablespoons orange juice
1 oz hazelnuts, chopped (25 g)

for the dressing:
4 tablespoons olive oil
1 tablespoon white wine vinegar
$\frac{1}{2}$ teaspoon English mustard powder
salt and freshly ground black pepper

Soak the raisins in the orange juice for 30 minutes or so. Make the dressing by whisking the olive oil, vinegar, mustard powder and salt and pepper together until well combined. Mix the grated carrots, courgettes and hazelnuts together in a large bowl and pour the dressing over, mixing well. Stir in the raisins and orange juice, and decorate with a few whole hazelnuts.
Serves 4–6.

CHICKEN AND AVOCADO SALAD

8–12 oz cold cooked chicken, cut into neat pieces (225–350 g)
1 ripe avocado
juice of ½ a lemon
2 tablespoons thick plain yogurt
few drops chilli sauce
salt and freshly ground black pepper

to serve:
lettuce leaves and paprika

Halve the avocado, remove the stone and scoop out the flesh. Mash it with the lemon juice, yogurt, chilli sauce and some salt and pepper. If you have a food processor, process it all together, until you have a thick green sauce. Place the chicken in a bowl, pour the dressing over, and mix well. Leave in the fridge for several hours to allow the flavours to develop. To serve, check the seasoning, adding more salt and pepper if necessary, give the salad a good stir, and then pile it into a serving bowl lined with lettuce leaves. Sprinkle a little paprika over the top. Serves 2–3.

CHICKEN AND PINEAPPLE SALAD

This works very well if you use a fresh pineapple; I suppose tinned pineapple would be OK but it wouldn't produce the same result.

8–12 oz cold cooked chicken (225–350 g)
12 oz fresh pineapple (350 g)
1 eating apple
juice of ½ a lemon
2 teaspoons soft brown sugar
3 tablespoons bought mayonnaise
1 tablespoon double cream
salt and freshly ground black pepper

to serve:
lettuce leaves

Cut the chicken into small neat pieces. Peel and core the pineapple and apple and cut into neat cubes. Place chicken, pineapple and apple in a bowl. Mix together the lemon juice, sugar, mayonnaise, cream and a little salt and pepper. Pour over the chicken, pineapple and apple and toss well. Line a salad bowl with lettuce leaves and pile the chicken and pineapple into the centre. This salad may be prepared a few hours before, but do not make it too far in advance as the juices run from the pineapple and the chicken goes soggy.
Serves 6.

CHICKEN LIVER SALAD

4 anchovies
a little milk
1 tablespoon sesame oil
4 oz chicken livers (110 g)
4 oz field mushrooms (110 g)
juice of $\frac{1}{2}$ a lemon
6 leaves endive
6 leaves lollo rosso or frisée lettuce
6 sprigs watercress
3 tablespoons olive oil
1 tablespoon white wine vinegar
salt and freshly ground black pepper

Start by leaving the anchovies to soak in a little milk to draw off their saltiness. Rinse and pat dry the chicken livers. Heat the sesame oil in a small frying pan and fry the livers until they are cooked. Remove with a slotted spoon and drain on kitchen paper. Add the mushrooms and lemon juice to the same pan and cook until the mushrooms are just tender. Chop the chicken livers quite finely and place in a large bowl. Add the mushrooms when they are cooked, together with the pan juices. Allow to go quite cold. When ready to assemble the salad, wash the endive, lollo rosso or frisée leaves, and watercress and shake dry. Tear into smallish pieces, and place in a bowl. Whisk the oil and vinegar together with some seasoning and pour over the leaves. Toss well. Pile the chicken livers and mushrooms in the centre, and decorate with the drained anchovies.
Serves 3–4.

CHINESE LEAF SALAD

1 head Chinese leaves
12 oz bean sprouts, washed (350 g)
2 red peppers, deseeded and cut into strips
2 oz unsalted peanuts (55 g)
1 tablespoon sesame seeds

for the dressing:
1 tablespoon sesame oil
5 tablespoons soy sauce
1 tablespoon runny honey
2 tablespoons white wine vinegar
salt and freshly ground black pepper

Blanch the bean sprouts for one minute in boiling water then drain. Leave to cool. Meanwhile, wash, dry, and shred the Chinese leaves. Mix together the leaves, bean sprouts, and red peppers. Put all the dressing ingredients into a screw-topped jar and shake vigorously until well combined. Stir into the salad bowl. Leave in a cool place to let the flavours develop for about an hour. Just before serving, stir in the peanuts and sprinkle the sesame seeds on top.
Serves 10.

CUCUMBER AND MINT SALAD

1 cucumber, peeled and sliced thinly
2–3 teaspoons salt
2 tablespoons fresh mint leaves, finely chopped
4 tablespoons thick natural yogurt
salt and freshly ground black pepper

to garnish:
1 teaspoon paprika and a few mint leaves

Put the sliced cucumber in a colander, sprinkle with the salt, and leave to drain for an hour or so. Rinse well in cold water, then pat dry on kitchen paper. Arrange the cucumber slices in overlapping circles around the outside of four smallish plates. Mix a little salt and pepper into the yogurt, stir in the mint, and then place a tablespoon in the centre of each cucumber ring. Sprinkle with paprika, pop a sprig of mint in the middle, and serve. If you can't get fresh mint, don't use dried, but try dried dill weed instead. Sour cream makes a pleasing alternative to yogurt. Serve with curries and spicy dishes.

FENNEL SALAD

4 oz long grain rice (110 g)
2 hard boiled eggs, quartered
1 bulb fennel, trimmed and thinly sliced
6 spring onions, trimmed and chopped
4 small tomatoes, quartered
8 black olives

for the vinaigrette dressing:
3 tablespoons olive oil
1 tablespoon white wine vinegar
salt and freshly ground black pepper
½ a teaspoon anchovy essence

to garnish:
1 tablespoon fresh chives, snipped

Put the rice on to cook in lightly salted boiling water. Drain the rice well, tip into a salad bowl, and leave to cool. Make the vinaigrette dressing by whisking all the ingredients together. Pour over the rice and mix well. Arrange the fennel, onions, eggs, tomatoes and black olives on top of the rice, and sprinkle the chives on top. Serve with crusty brown rolls. This dish goes very well with fish, or, if you are serving it by itself, arrange six to eight anchovy fillets, briefly soaked in milk, on top of the fennel and eggs.

FETA AND WATERMELON SALAD

½ a ripe watermelon
8 oz feta cheese (225 g)
12 black Greek olives, stoned
red frisée or radicchio leaves

for the dressing:
3 tablespoons olive oil
1 tablespoon white wine vinegar or lemon juice
freshly ground black pepper

Cut the rind off the water melon and remove its seeds. Cut into smallish chunks. Chop the feta cheese into similar sized pieces. Mix the cheese and melon with the olives. Rinse and pat dry the frisée or radicchio leaves. Whisk or shake the dressing ingredients together, then pour over the cheese and water melon and toss well. You shouldn't need any salt in the dressing as the feta is already quite salty. Line a large salad bowl or four small bowls with the leaves, and pile the cheese and melon into the centre. Serve at once with hot pitta bread.

GOATS CHEESE SALAD

A generous amount of strongly flavoured salad leaves, including frisée, radicchio and endive
3 inner celery stalks, chopped
1 tablespoon walnuts, chopped
4 small or 2 large, halved, round goats' cheeses
4 slices French bread

for the vinaigrette dressing:
2 tablespoons walnut oil
2 tablespoons olive oil
1 tablespoon white wine vinegar
salt and freshly ground black pepper

Wash the salad leaves well and pat dry. Remove the strings from the celery with a vegetable peeler, then cut into matchstick strips. Line four medium plates with the leaves, then sprinkle the celery and walnuts on top. Mix together the vinaigrette ingredients, check the seasoning, and pour over the salad. Now toast the bread on one side only, turn each slice over and top with a round of goat's cheese. Replace under the grill until the cheese just begins to melt, then place each hot toast in the middle of the salad and serve at once.

HOT CRAB SALAD

10 oz crab meat, fresh, frozen, or tinned (280 g)
3–4 inner sticks celery, washed
1 medium green pepper, deseeded
4 spring onions
4 tablespoons mayonnaise
1 teaspoon Worcester sauce
salt and freshly ground black pepper
4 oz prawns or shrimps (110 g)
4 tablespoons fresh white breadcrumbs

Cut the vegetables into slim diagonal pieces, and mix with the mayonnaise, Worcester sauce, salt and pepper to taste, crab meat, prawns, and half the breadcrumbs. Spoon into a shallow baking dish and sprinkle the rest of the breadcrumbs on top. Bake in a pre-heated oven at Gas 4, 350 deg F, 180 deg C for 20–25 minutes until heated through, and serve at once. You can also cook this dish in four individual gratin dishes, in which case, cook it for 15–20 minutes.

ITALIAN SALMON SALAD

14 oz tin flageolet beans (400 g)
14 oz tin cannellini beans (400 g)
7 oz tin salmon (200 g)
2 inch piece of cucumber, peeled (5 cm)
6 spring onions, chopped
12 black olives, stoned

for the dressing:
3 tablespoons olive oil
1 tablespoon white wine vinegar
salt and freshly ground black pepper
$\frac{1}{4}$ teaspoon dried basil or 1 teaspoon fresh chopped leaves

Drain and rinse the beans, then combine them in a salad bowl. Drain the salmon and flake it, then add to the beans. Dice the cucumber and stir it and the chopped spring onions into the bowl. Shake or whisk the dressing ingredients together until well mixed, then pour over the salad, stir gently, and leave for an hour or two before serving to allow the flavours to develop.
Serves 6.

ITALIAN WINTER SALAD

1 lb leeks, whites only (450 g)
1 small cauliflower, washed
8 oz broccoli, washed (225 g)
8 oz carrots, scrubbed (225 g)
4 inner celery sticks, scrubbed

for the dressing:
2 tablespoons fresh lemon juice
6 tablespoons olive oil
1 teaspoon English mustard powder
salt and freshly ground black pepper

Slice the leeks into 1 inch (2.5 cm) lengths. Break the cauliflower and broccoli into florets. Slice the carrots and celery. Steam all the vegetables until tender, or boil them in the minimum of lightly salted boiling water. Do not overcook; the vegetables need to have some "bite" to them. Meanwhile, whisk together the lemon juice, olive oil, salt, pepper and mustard powder, and, when the vegetables are ready, drain them if necessary, then toss them in the dressing while they are still hot. Place in a warmed serving dish and serve warm.
Serves 4–6.

LEAFY GREEN SALAD

1 large crisp lettuce
8 spinach leaves
8 lollo rosso, radicchio, or endive leaves
3 sorrel leaves
½ a cucumber, thinly sliced
6 spring onions, chopped, or 1 red onion, peeled and thinly sliced
10 walnuts, chopped

for the dressing:
¼ pint olive oil (150 ml)
2 tablespoons white wine vinegar
2 tablespoons fresh parsley, chopped
salt and freshly ground black pepper

Wash the leaves well, dry them in a clean tea towel or salad spinner, then tear them into smallish pieces. Mix them well in a very large bowl, and add the walnuts, cucumber and spring onions or onion. Mix all the dressing ingredients together. Taste to judge the right amount of vinegar, salt and pepper; the dressing should be on the oily side, but with just the right amount of sharpness. Pour over the leaves just before serving and toss well. Do not be tempted to dress the leaves too soon, or they will wilt. This is quite a large salad, so it is a good idea just to dress the amount of leaves you think people will eat; the rest of the prepared leaves and the dressing will keep very well, separately, in the fridge for several days.
Serves 8.

ORANGE AND PEANUT COLESLAW

This is a good variation on the traditional coleslaw and is a useful addition to a buffet party table.

1 lb crisp white cabbage (450 g)
3 oranges, halved, peeled and with pith removed
2 oz salted peanuts (55 g)
for the dressing:
4 tablespoons olive oil
2 tablespoons white wine vinegar
$\frac{1}{2}$ teaspoon mustard powder
1 teaspoon celery seeds
1 teaspoon sugar
freshly ground black pepper

Shred the cabbage very finely and place in a large bowl. Tear the oranges into segments over the bowl to catch the juice, then stir the segments into the cabbage. Mix in the peanuts. To make the dressing, whisk the oil, vinegar, celery seeds, mustard powder, sugar and pepper together until well combined, then pour over the cabbage. Toss well. Leave for a couple of hours to allow the flavours to develop. Serves 6.

POTATO, CELERY AND WALNUT SALAD

12 oz peeled or scraped salad potatoes, cooked (350 g)
6 inner stalks celery, scrubbed
1 oz walnuts, chopped (25 g)
2 inch piece cucumber, diced (5 cm)
6 spring onions, whites only, chopped
3 tablespoons mayonnaise
2 tablespoons thick plain yogurt
1 tablespoon lemon juice
1 tablespoon fresh parsley, chopped
salt and freshly ground black pepper

to garnish:
paprika or sprigs of fresh parsley

Cut the potatoes into evenly sized pieces. Wash and chop the celery. Mix potatoes, celery and walnuts together with the chopped cucumber and spring onions. In another bowl, mix together the mayonnaise, yogurt, lemon juice, parsley and some salt and pepper. Stir into the salad, mixing well but gently. Leave for a couple of hours in the fridge for the flavours to develop and garnish with parsley or sprinkle with paprika before serving.

SEAFOOD SALAD

2 fat scallops
6 oz shelled prawns (175 g)
6 oz shelled mussels (175 g)
1 inch chunk cucumber (2.5 cm)
2 tablespoons natural yogurt
1 tablespoon double cream
1 tablespoon tomato purée
1 tablespoon lemon juice
1 tablespoon creamed horseradish
salt and freshly ground black pepper

to serve:
lettuce, watercress, and lemon wedges

Slice the scallops thinly and mix with the prawns and mussels. Cut the cucumber into slivers and mix in. Now beat together the yogurt, cream, tomato purée, lemon juice, creamed horseradish, salt and pepper, and pour over the fish and cucumber. Stir gently. Serve on a bed of shredded lettuce and watercress and garnish with lemon wedges.

TARRAGON PORK SALAD

12 oz lean pork tenderloin (350 g)
4 tablespoons sunflower oil
2 tablespoons orange juice
2 tablespoons fresh tarragon, chopped
salt and freshly ground black pepper
8 oz small new potatoes, washed (225 g)
4 oz French beans (110 g)
6 cherry tomatoes, halved

for the dressing:
3 tablespoons olive oil
1 tablespoon orange juice
1 teaspoon runny honey
2 teaspoons fresh tarragon, chopped

Cut the pork into $\frac{1}{4}$ inch (0.5 cm) slices and lay it in a shallow dish. Mix the oil, orange juice, tarragon and seasoning together and pour over the pork. Cover and leave to marinate for 3–4 hours. Boil the potatoes in their skins, drain, and leave to cool. Top and tail the French beans, cut into 1 inch (2.5 cm) lengths, and blanch in boiling lightly salted water for 5 minutes. Drain and allow to cool. Remove the pork from the marinade, reserving the juices. Barbecue or grill the pork until cooked, turning it once, and brushing with the marinade. Mix the potatoes, French beans and tomatoes together. Whisk the dressing ingredients together with some salt and pepper and pour over the potato salad. To serve, arrange the pork slices around the edge of a serving plate, and put the salad in the centre.
Serves 2–3.

TOMATO SALAD

If you grow your own tomatoes, you've probably got some with flavour, but otherwise you should buy tomatoes from Provence or Italy if you can get them, because commercial Dutch and English varieties have no flavour and render this salad pointless.

1 lb ripe tomatoes (450 g)
1 red onion
6 black olives, stoned

for the dressing:
3 tablespoons olive oil
1 tablespoon white wine vinegar
salt and freshly ground black pepper
1 tablespoon fresh basil leaves, chopped

to garnish:
fresh basil leaves or Mozzarella cheese

Try to get Italian tomatoes, or French ones from Provence, as English ones tend to be tasteless. Wash and dry them, then cut into quarters. Peel and slice the red onion. Place tomatoes, onion and olives in a large bowl and mix gently. Whisk all the dressing ingredients together, or shake in a screw topped jar, and pour over the tomatoes. Toss gently and serve at once, garnished with basil leaves or a few slivers of Mozzarella cheese.

TURKEY AND APPLE SALAD

10–12 oz cold cooked turkey, cubed (275–350 g)
2 apples, cored and sliced
4 tender celery stalks, washed and sliced
4 spring onions, chopped
1 oz broken walnuts (25 g)
lettuce leaves

for the dressing:
1 tablespoon cranberry sauce
5 fl oz thick natural yogurt (150 ml)
1 tablespoon lemon juice
1 teaspoon caster sugar
1 tablespoon parsley, chopped
¼ teaspoon English mustard powder
salt and freshly ground black pepper

Mix together the turkey, apples, celery and spring onions. Whisk together the cranberry sauce, yogurt, lemon juice, sugar, parsley, mustard powder and salt and pepper, then pour over the turkey and apple mixture, and toss well. Line a bowl or salad platter with washed and dried lettuce leaves, and pile the salad in the centre. Scatter the broken walnuts over the top. (If you use red apples and one of the red-leaved varieties of lettuce, this salad looks particularly attractive.)

WALDORF SALAD

1 lb eating apples (450 g)
4 inner celery stalks, washed
2 oz walnuts, chopped (55 g)
$\frac{1}{4}$ pint mayonnaise (150 ml)
juice of $\frac{1}{2}$ a lemon
$\frac{1}{2}$ teaspoon sugar
salt and freshly ground black pepper

to serve:
lettuce leaves
1 eating apple
a few walnut halves

Peel and core the apples and cut into dice. Mix in a bowl with the celery and walnuts. Beat the mayonnaise with the lemon juice, sugar and some salt and pepper, add to the salad and toss well. Line a salad bowl with washed and dried lettuce leaves and pile the salad into the centre; core and slice the eating apple and use as a garnish together with a few walnut halves.

WATERCRESS AND MUSHROOM SALAD

1 bunch watercress, washed and dried
4 oz button mushrooms (110 g)
6 large Cos lettuce leaves

for the dressing:
3 tablespoons olive oil
1 tablespoon white wine vinegar
1 teaspoon Dijon mustard
1 teaspoon runny honey
salt and freshly ground black pepper

Wash and pat dry the lettuce and tear the leaves into smallish pieces; wash the watercress and chop roughly. Wipe the mushrooms and slice thinly. Mix together in a salad bowl. Whisk the dressing ingredients until well combined, then pour over the salad, and leave to stand for 30–40 minutes before serving so that the mushrooms soak up the honey and mustard flavours.

PUDDINGS

Blackcurrant · Chocolate · Pear · Ginger · Apple · Strawberry

PUDDINGS

Puddings in our busy house tend to be fruit and yogurt; but in the winter I might cheer everyone up with a huge steamed ginger pudding or a baked apple and almond pudding, or in the summer I will make my very favourite summer pudding with sweet, sharp, freshly-picked fruit.

Dinner parties call for a couple of delicious puds; but they don't have to be complicated. The more successful and high powered your guests are, the more they are likely to go weak at the knees at the sight of a hot, flaky pastry apple pie served with lashings of cream.

One of my favourites here is tiramisu. It became rather a fashionable pud a couple of years ago, so all the food writers scorn it now, but I don't care, it's staying in my repertoire because it is so scrumptious. Tiramisu is supposed to be Italian for "pick me up". It's full of brandy, cream cheese and chocolate, so it's actually more likely to make you collapse under the table, but once in a while, who cares?

Apple and almond pudding
Apricot Dacquoise (nutty meringue gateau)
Apricot pancakes
Blackcurrant ice cream
Blackcurrant strudel
Chestnut and chocolate roulade
Chocolate orange mousse
Chocolate pears
Chocolate strawberry roll
Christmas meringue
Christmas pudding
Compôte of pears
Custard ice cream
German apple slice

Oriental fruit salad
Pear and ginger tart
Raspberry and redcurrant tart
Raspberry Malakoff
Raspberry roll
Redcurrant and almond roulade
Rhubarb fool
Steamed ginger pudding
Summer meringue
Summer pudding
Tiramisu (Italian chocolate and brandy trifle)
Tropical fruit pavlova
Vanilla ice cream
Walnut tart

APPLE AND ALMOND PUDDING

for the base:
$1\frac{1}{2}$ lb apples, peeled, cored and sliced (700 g)
2 tablespoons sugar

for the topping:
2 eggs, beaten
4 oz self raising flour (110 g)
2 oz ground almonds (55 g)
4 oz soft margarine at room temperature (110 g)
4 oz caster sugar (110 g)
2–3 tablespoons milk
2–3 drops almond essence
1 oz flaked almonds (25 g)

Sift the flour and ground almonds together then beat them with all the topping ingredients except the flaked almonds, adding enough milk to give a soft dropping consistency. Arrange the sliced apple in the base of a large shallow ovenproof dish and sprinkle the sugar over the top. Spoon the topping mixture over the apples, then sprinkle with the flaked almonds. Bake at Gas 5, 375 deg F, 190 deg C for 40–45 minutes, until nicely risen and golden brown. Serve hot or cold.
Serves 6–8.

APRICOT DACQUOISE
Nutty meringue gateau

the whites of 4 large fresh eggs
8 oz caster sugar (225 g)
2 oz almonds or hazelnuts, blanched and finely chopped (55 g)
8 oz dried apricots, soaked overnight (225 g)
2–4 oz sugar (55–110 g)
$\frac{1}{2}$ a cinnamon stick
$\frac{1}{2}$ pint double cream (300 ml)

to decorate:
whole almonds or hazelnuts

Whisk the egg whites until stiff, then gradually whisk in the caster sugar. Gently fold in the nuts, then divide the mixture between two baking trays lined with non-stick parchment, forming circles about 8 inches (20 cm) in diameter. Bake at Gas 2, 300 deg F, 150 deg C, for 1 hour, then switch off the oven and leave the meringues to dry out, preferably overnight. Next day, heat the apricots in a little water, with sugar to taste and the cinnamon. Simmer for 5–10 minutes until the fruit is soft, then drain and allow to cool. (Remove the cinnamon stick and serve the cooking liquor, laced with some brandy, as a pouring sauce.) Roughly chop the apricots. Whisk the cream until stiff and spread about two-thirds on one of the meringues. Arrange the apricots on top, cover with the other meringue, and decorate with the rest of the cream and some whole nuts.
Serves 6–8.

APRICOT PANCAKES

for the batter:
4 oz plain flour (110 g)
1 teaspoon icing sugar
2 eggs, beaten
½ pint milk (300 ml)
grated zest of ½ a lemon
olive oil and butter for frying

for the filling:
8 oz ready-to-cook dried apricots (225 g)
juice of ½ a lemon
1–2 tablespoons sugar, to taste

To make the pancakes, sift the flour and sugar into a large bowl, make a well in the centre, add the eggs and half the milk, and gradually whisk in the flour and sugar. When you have a smooth batter, add the rest of the milk and the lemon zest. Heat a little oil and butter in a frying pan and when sizzling hot, tip in a tablespoon or so of the batter. Fry on a high heat on both sides, then tip the pancake out and keep warm. Make 10 more pancakes in the same way. While you are cooking the pancakes, put the apricots in a saucepan with the lemon juice, caster sugar and enough water just to cover. Stew, covered, until soft, then drain, reserving any juices, and process until a smooth purée is obtained. Divide between the pancakes, roll them up, and serve at once. Offer any remaining apricot juice separately.

BLACKCURRANT ICE CREAM

1 lb fresh blackcurrants (450 g)
8 oz sugar (225 g)
½ pint single cream (300 ml)
yolks of two large fresh eggs
3 tablespoons caster sugar
½ pint double cream (300 ml)

Strip the fruit from the stalks, wash, and put into a pan with the 8 oz (225 g) sugar. Simmer for 10–15 minutes until soft. Sieve. Heat the single cream to boiling point, and meanwhile whisk the egg yolks and caster sugar together until thick and creamy, then pour in the hot cream. Stir well. Return to the pan and stir with a wooden spoon over a gentle heat until the custard will coat the back of the spoon. Do not boil. Take off the heat and leave to cool. Stir in the sieved blackcurrants. Beat the double cream until thick but not stiff, then fold it in. Pour into a clean container and freeze for a couple of hours. Then beat again to break up the ice crystals. Freeze again. Before eating, allow to soften in the fridge for an hour or so. Serve with langue du chat biscuits.
Serves 6–8.

BLACKCURRANT STRUDEL

8 oz blackcurrants, washed and stripped (225 g)
1 tablespoon fresh brown breadcrumbs
4 oz sugar (110 g)
½ teaspoon ground cinnamon
8 oz filo pastry leaves, defrosted (225 g)
1 oz butter (25 g)
1 tablespoon runny honey
¼ pint water (150 ml)

Mix together the blackcurrants, breadcrumbs, sugar and cinnamon. Fold each pastry leaf in half across its shorter side, place a tablespoon of the blackcurrant mixture near one end, fold in the sides, then roll up. Work swiftly or the filo pastry will start to dry out. Place in a baking dish greased with some of the butter. When you have made all the little parcels and packed them in a single layer into the baking dish, dot them with the remaining butter and bake for 25–30 minutes at Gas 6, 400 deg F, 200 deg C, until lightly browned. Make a syrup with the honey and water by boiling them together until thickened, then pour over the hot strudels. Serve hot or cold, with cream.

CHESTNUT AND CHOCOLATE ROULADE

for the roulade:
3 large fresh eggs, separated
3 oz caster sugar (75 g)
1 oz cocoa, sifted (25 g)

for the filling:
¼ pint double cream (150 ml)
8 oz unsweetened chestnut purée (225 g)
2 tablespoons Grand Marnier or similar
2 tablespoons icing sugar

To make the roulade, whisk the egg yolks with the sugar until thick. Carefully fold in the cocoa powder. Whisk the egg whites in a large, clean bowl until stiff. Stir one tablespoonful into the cocoa mixture to slacken it, then gently fold in the remaining egg whites. Pour into a greased and lined Swiss roll tin and bake at Gas 4, 350 deg F, 180 deg C for 15–20 minutes. When the cake feels springy to the touch, take it out of the oven, cover with a clean damp tea towel and leave overnight. To fill, whisk the cream until thick. Beat the chestnut purée with the Grand Marnier and icing sugar, then stir into the cream. Liberally sprinkle icing sugar over a piece of greaseproof paper and tip the roulade out on to it. Spread the chestnut mixture over the top then carefully roll up. Don't worry if it cracks; it all adds to the effect. Sprinkle with icing sugar before serving.
Serves 6–8.

CHOCOLATE ORANGE MOUSSE

1 Seville orange
½ oz powdered gelatine (15 g)
2 large fresh eggs, separated
3 whole fresh eggs
3 oz caster sugar (75 g)
7 oz plain chocolate (200 g)
2 fl oz water (55 ml)
3 fl oz double cream (75 ml)

to decorate:
¼ pint double cream (150 ml)
chocolate curls

Grate the zest and squeeze the juice from the orange. Soak the gelatine in the orange juice in a small bowl, then place in a pan of hot water until dissolved and completely transparent. Meanwhile, place the three whole eggs with the two egg yolks and the caster sugar in a bowl placed over a pan of barely simmering water. Whisk until the mixture is really thick and creamy. Then remove the bowl from the heat and place another bowl over the hot water, break the chocolate into it, add the water, and stir until the chocolate melts. Remove from the heat, stir in the grated orange zest, and leave to cool. Push the gelatine through a strainer to make sure there are no lumps in it, then mix it with the chocolate and egg mixtures. Whisk the egg whites to the soft peak stage and fold them into the mixture carefully. Whip the double cream and fold in. Pour into a 2 pint (1 litre) soufflé dish, cover, and chill for several hours. To decorate, whip the double cream until thick, and pipe on top and then sprinkle with chocolate curls.

CHOCOLATE PEARS

4 firm pears
juice of 1 orange
1 oz nuts, finely chopped (25 g)

for the sauce:
1½ oz butter (40 g)
1½ oz drinking chocolate (40 g)
1 tablespoon golden syrup
finely grated zest of 1 orange

Peel and core the pears and poach them gently in the orange juice until soft. Remove the pears to a warmed serving dish, and bring the orange and pear juices in the pan to the boil and reduce to one tablespoonful. Turn down the heat and add the butter, drinking chocolate, golden syrup and orange zest, and allow the butter to melt. Stir well until the sauce is velvety smooth. Pour over the pears, sprinkle with the chopped nuts, and serve at once.

CHOCOLATE STRAWBERRY ROLL

for the roll:
3 fresh eggs
4 oz caster sugar (110 g)
4 oz plain flour, sifted (110 g)
1 tablespoon cocoa powder, sifted
caster sugar, for dredging

for the filling:
6 oz strawberries (75 g)
½ pint double cream (300 ml)

Line a Swiss roll tin with baking parchment. Beat the eggs and caster sugar together in a bowl set over a pan of hot water. When the mixture is thick and creamy, remove from the heat and continue to beat until cool. Sift in half the flour and fold in lightly. Sift and fold in the rest of the flour and cocoa powder, then lightly fold in a tablespoon of hot water. Pour the mixture into the tin and tip it gently so that it runs evenly into the corners. Bake at Gas 6, 400 deg F, 200 deg C, for 10–12 minutes until risen and golden brown. Meanwhile, cover a clean damp tea towel with baking parchment, and sprinkle with caster sugar. When the roll is cooked, carefully turn it out on to the parchment. Roll it up loosely lengthways, then transfer to a wire rack to cool. When cold, whip the cream and slice the strawberries. Unroll the cake and spread the cream on it then add the strawberries and roll the whole thing up again, dredging with caster sugar.
Serves 6.

CHRISTMAS MERINGUE

for the meringue:
3 large egg whites
6 oz caster sugar (175 g)

for the topping:
8 oz chestnut purée (225 g)
1 tablespoon icing sugar
1 tablespoon brandy
4 oz Brazil nuts, chopped (110 g)
½ pint double cream (300 ml)
2 oz dark plain chocolate, grated (55 g)

Whisk the egg whites until stiff, then whisk in the sugar a spoonful at a time. Mark out an 8 inch (20 cm) circle on a sheet of baking parchment, place on a baking tray, and spread the meringue over the parchment, building up the sides. Bake at Gas 1, 275 deg F, 140 deg C, for one hour, then leave in the oven until dried out (preferably overnight.) To serve, combine the chestnut purée with the icing sugar and brandy, and spread over the meringue. Sprinkle with the nuts. Whip the cream, and pipe or spread it over the top, and sprinkle with grated chocolate.
Serves 6.

CHRISTMAS PUDDING

12 oz currants (350 g)
12 oz seedless raisins (350 g)
12 oz sultanas (350 g)
12 oz fresh white breadcrumbs (350 g)
4 oz mixed nuts, such as almonds, hazelnuts, pecans, brazils, walnuts, chopped (110 g)
4 oz demerara sugar (110 g)
grated zest of 1 orange
grated zest of 1 lemon
1 teaspoon ground cinnamon
1 teaspoon nutmeg, freshly grated
8 oz butter, melted (225 g)
6 fl oz brandy or whisky (175 ml)
¼ pint milk (150 ml)
4 large eggs

Place all the dry ingredients in a large bowl and mix well together. In another bowl, whisk together the melted butter, brandy or whisky, milk and eggs. Pour this liquid into the dry ingredients, and mix well.

Turn the mixture into one large or two smaller pudding basins, leaving a good 1 inch (2.5 cm) at the top. Cover with buttered greaseproof paper and foil tied tightly with string, or with a tight-fitting lid, and stand each basin in a saucepan. Pour boiling water into the saucepan to come about half way up its sides. Bring back to the boil, lower the heat to a simmer, cover, and steam for 6 hours. Check from time to time and top up with more hot water if needed.

Cool, then place clean greaseproof paper on top of the puddings before storing. On Christmas Day, or when needed, steam for at least 2 hours.
Note: the size of the pudding does not alter the cooking times. Longer cooking just makes the pudding darker.
Serves about 20.

COMPOTE OF PEARS

6 large slightly under-ripe pears
1½ pints water (850 ml)
4 oz sugar (110 g)
½ pint sweet white wine (300 ml)
1 tablespoon Kirsch (optional)

Put the sugar and water into a saucepan and bring to the boil. Bubble for five minutes, then add the wine. Bring back to the boil. Meanwhile, peel, quarter and core the pears. Place them in the syrup and turn down the heat. Poach the pears gently until tender. Remove with a slotted spoon and lay the pears in a shallow serving dish. Bring the liquid back to the boil, and reduce to about ⅓ pint (190 ml). Pour over the pears and leave to cool. Add the Kirsch, if using, just before serving. (You can cook apples, apricots and peaches in the same way.)
Serves 6.

CUSTARD ICE CREAM

1 pint milk (600 ml)
3 oz caster sugar (75 g)
1 oz plain flour, sifted (25 g)
1 egg
½ teaspoon vanilla essence
1 oz unsalted butter, cut into small pieces (25 g)

Beat the milk, sugar, flour, egg and vanilla essence together until well blended. Pour into a saucepan and, stirring all the time, bring to the boil and then simmer for two or three minutes, still stirring to stop it sticking. Take off the heat when it is nice and thick, and add the butter. Stir until it melts, then pour into a shallow container, cool, and pop into the freezer. After a couple of hours, the ice cream will start to freeze around the edge; take it out, whisk it for 30 seconds, and replace in the freezer. Before consuming leave to soften in the fridge for 20 minutes. This is good served with sliced bananas and chopped nuts.
Serves 4–6.

GERMAN APPLE SLICE

for the filling:
1½ lb cooking apples (700 g)
2 oz mixed dried fruit (55 g)
2 oz soft brown sugar (55 g)
¼ teaspoon each ground cinnamon, cloves and nutmeg
grated zest and juice of ½ a lemon
2 tablespoons fresh brown breadcrumbs

for the pastry:
6 oz plain flour, sifted (175 g)
4 oz unsalted butter at room temperature (110 g)
3 or 4 tablespoons milk

Peel, core and slice the apples and place in a bowl with the dried fruit, sugar, spices, lemon zest and juice, and breadcrumbs. Stir well. Now make the pastry. Rub in the flour and butter (you can use margarine, but it's not as nice), and then add enough milk to form a pliable dough. Roll out on a floured surface to form a rectangle measuring about 16 × 12 inches (45 × 30 cm). Spoon the apple mixture down the centre of the pastry, leaving a margin of about 2 inches (5 cm) on all sides. Fold the sides over the top of the apple mixture, leaving a gap down the middle, then brush with milk. Slide carefully on to a greased baking sheet, and bake for 40–50 minutes at Gas 4, 350 deg F, 180 deg C. Serve cut into slices, hot or cold.
Serves 6.

ORIENTAL FRUIT SALAD

1 fresh ripe mango
4 kiwi fruit
4 pieces stem ginger
4 tablespoons ginger syrup

Peel the mango and cut into four, removing the stone. Taste the outer flesh and if it is bitter, slice it off and discard it. Slice the sweet mango flesh. Peel the kiwi fruit and slice. Slice the ginger. Pour a tablespoon of ginger syrup on to four dessert plates, then divide the fruits and ginger between each plate and arrange attractively. You could also add some thin slices of fresh pineapple or experiment with other exotic fruits. This is a very good pudding to follow a Chinese meal, and doesn't need cream or anything else to go with it.

PEAR AND GINGER TART

for the pastry:
1 teaspoon ground ginger
6 oz plain flour, sifted (175 g)
3 oz margarine or butter (75 g)
1 oz soft brown sugar (25 g)
cold water to mix

for the filling:
1½ lb pears (700 g)
3 tablespoons ginger syrup taken from a jar of stem ginger
1 tablespoon soft brown sugar

Make the pastry in the usual way: sift the flour and ginger together, rub in the fat, then stir in the sugar and add enough cold water to make a soft but not sticky dough. Leave to rest for 30 minutes. Meanwhile, peel, quarter and core the pears and place in a saucepan with the ginger syrup and tablespoon of sugar. Cover and simmer very gently until the pears are soft but not mushy. Remove the pears from the cooking liquid. Reserve the liquid and slice the pears. Roll out the pastry to fit a 9 inch (23 cm) metal flan tin and bake blind at Gas 6, 400 deg F, 200 deg C, for 12 minutes. Remove from the oven and fill with overlapping rings of the sliced pears. Return to the oven and bake for 20 minutes at Gas 4, 350 deg F, 180 deg C. Meanwhile, boil the pear cooking liquid hard until it reduces by about half and looks thick and syrupy, then pour over the cooked hot tart to form a glaze. Serve with cream, plain yogurt, or custard.
Serves 6–8.

RASPBERRY AND REDCURRANT TART

for the pastry:
6 oz plain flour, sifted (175 g)
4 oz butter or margarine (110 g)
1 egg
2 oz caster sugar (55 g)

for the filling:
1½ lb raspberries (700 g)
½ lb redcurrants, de-stalked (225 g)
6 oz sugar (175 g)
1 tablespoon redcurrant jelly

Quickly rub in the flour and fat, add the sugar and stir in the egg. Work the dough as little as possible. Leave it in the fridge for an hour or so, then roll it out and line a ten inch (25 cm) flan tin. Bake blind at Gas 4, 350 deg F, 180 deg C for 20 minutes. While it is cooking, simmer the fruit in the sugar with 3–4 tablespoons of water. The fruit should be soft but not allowed to lose its shape. Drain, reserving the juices. When the pastry case is cool, fill it with the fruit. Add the redcurrant jelly to the fruit juices, and heat, stirring all the time, until the juices reduce and you have a thick syrup. Brush this over the fruit and allow to cool. Serve cold. Serves 6.

RASPBERRY MALAKOFF

3 tablespoons Kirsch
8 oz fresh raspberries (225 g)

to decorate:
¼ pint double cream (150 ml)
12 raspberries
12 whole blanched almonds

1 large packet boudoir biscuits

for the filling:
6 oz unsalted butter (175 g)
6 oz caster sugar (175 g)
6 oz ground almonds (175 g)
½ pint double cream (300 ml)

Beat the butter and sugar together until pale. In another bowl, whip the ½ pint (300 ml) cream until quite stiff. Mix the ground almonds into the sugar and butter mixture, then stir in the Kirsch. Finally add the cream and the raspberries, mixing well but without crushing the raspberries. Line a soufflé dish or loose-bottomed cake tin with greaseproof paper, and brush it lightly with oil. Stand the biscuits up around the edge of the dish, sugar sides outwards. Spoon the raspberry mixture into the middle and press down with the back of a wooden spoon. Leave in the fridge overnight or for at least 4 hours. Using a serrated knife, trim the tops of the biscuits so that they come to the same level as the raspberry filling. Turn the whole pudding out, upside down, on to a serving plate, and peel off the greaseproof paper. Decorate with swirls of whipped cream, extra raspberries, and blanched almonds.
Serves 6–8.

REDCURRANT AND ALMOND ROULADE

This is a good pudding for summer entertaining, because it looks lovely and tastes wonderful, but it's actually quite easy to prepare. If the roulade cracks when you roll it up, it doesn't matter, as the top is sprinkled with icing sugar and decorated with tiny sprigs of redcurrants and flaked almonds.

for the roulade:
6 fresh eggs
8 oz caster sugar (225 g)
4 oz ground almonds (110 g)
1 oz plain flour, sifted (25 g)
few drops almond essence

for the filling:
$\frac{1}{2}$ pint double cream (300 ml)
2–3 tablespoons caster sugar
6 oz redcurrants, stripped weight (175 g)

to decorate:
icing sugar, sifted
3–4 sprigs redcurrants
blanched flaked almonds

Separate the eggs into two large bowls. Whisk the egg whites until stiff. Beat the yolks with the caster sugar until pale and creamy, then mix in the ground almonds and sifted flour. Add a few drops of almond essence. Stir in one or two tablespoons of the whisked egg white to slacken the stiff yolk mixture, then fold in the rest of the egg white.

Pour the mixture into a Swiss roll tin lined with baking parchment; let the paper come well up and a little above the sides of the tin, as the mixture rises quite a lot when cooking. Bake at Gas 4, 350 deg F, 180 deg C, for 25–30 minutes or until golden brown. Remove from the oven, turn out on to a wire rack covered with a slightly damp clean tea towel, allow to rest for a couple of minutes, then carefully peel off the baking parchment.

When ready to serve, whip the cream until stiff. Trim the edges of the sponge and place on a board sprinkled liberally with sifted icing sugar, then spread the cream on to the sponge and sprinkle with caster sugar and redcurrants. Roll up carefully; don't worry if it cracks. Sprinkle with icing sugar, redcurrants and flaked almonds. Serves 6.

RHUBARB FOOL

1 lb young rhubarb, washed (450 g)
2 tablespoons soft brown sugar
1 teaspoon lemon juice
½ pint double cream (300 ml)
¼ pint thick natural yogurt (150 ml)

Cut the rhubarb into one inch (2.5 cm) pieces and put into a saucepan with a close-fitting lid together with the sugar and lemon juice and simmer very gently until the rhubarb is tender. Leave to cool, then whip the cream until thick. Gently stir together the yogurt, cream and rhubarb; do not mix too much or the rhubarb will become mushy. Divide between six tall dishes or glasses, and serve cold. (For a change, add a little chopped stem ginger, or the zest of half an orange and a teaspoon of orange juice.)
Serves 6.

STEAMED GINGER PUDDING

4 oz self raising flour, sifted (110 g)
¼ teaspoon baking powder
1 teaspoon ground ginger
2 oz soft margarine, at room temperature (55 g)
2 oz caster sugar (55 g)
1 egg, lightly beaten
1 or 2 tablespoons milk
2 tablespoons golden syrup
a little extra margarine for greasing

Put a large saucepan one third filled with water on to boil. Sift the flour, baking powder and ginger into a large bowl, then add the margarine, sugar and egg. Beat with an electric beater or a wooden spoon for one or two minutes until well blended, adding enough milk to obtain a smooth dropping consistency. Grease a 1 pint (600 ml) pudding basin, then spoon the golden syrup into the base. Pour the batter into the basin, smooth the top, and cover with a lid or greaseproof paper, well tied down. Steam for about 1¼ hours, adding an extra 15 minutes or so if you have used wholemeal flour. To serve, tip the pudding out on to a flat plate and serve piping hot with custard or ice cream.

SUMMER MERINGUE

for the meringue:
4 egg whites
8 oz caster sugar (225 g)
for the topping:
4 oz raspberries (110 g)
4 oz redcurrants, stripped (110 g)
4 oz caster sugar (110 g)
½ pint whipping cream (300 ml)

Whisk the egg whites until stiff, then whisk in the sugar in spoonfuls. Spoon the meringue out on to a baking sheet covered with baking parchment and make a circle about nine inches (22 cm) in diameter with slightly raised edges. Bake at Gas ¼, 225 deg F, 110 deg C, for about 4 hours or until dry. Leave in the oven overnight if possible, then keep in an airtight tin. Two or three hours before serving, very gently soften the redcurrants with half the caster sugar; don't let the fruit become too mushy. Allow to cool. Stir in the raspberries. When ready to serve, whip the cream, stir in the remaining 2 oz (55 g) sugar, pile the cream on to the meringue and gently spoon the fruit on top. If there's any juice left from the fruit, serve it separately.

SUMMER PUDDING

4 oz small ripe strawberries (110 g)
4 oz redcurrants, stripped weight (110 g)
4 oz blackcurrants, stripped weight (110 g)
8 oz raspberries (225 g)
2 tablespoons water (225 g)
4 oz caster sugar (110 g)
5 or 6 slices day old white bread
butter

Put the washed fruit, sugar and water into a saucepan and stew very gently until the sugar has dissolved and the fruit is soft. Do not overcook. Meanwhile, cut the crusts off the bread and butter it. Butter a 1 lb (450 g) pudding basin and line it with the bread, butter side outside. Cut the bread to fit, fill in any small gaps, and leave some bread over for a lid. Pour the hot cooked fruit into the basin, reserving some of the juice if there is a lot. Now fit the rest of the bread on to the fruit, butter side uppermost, and put a plate or saucer on top and some weights on top of that. Leave in the fridge for 6–8 hours. The bread should soak up all the juices; if there are any white patches, tip in the reserved juices. To serve, carefully invert the pudding on to a serving plate, and offer with pouring cream. (Tip the pud out just before serving, otherwise the weight of the fruit tends to make it collapse.) Serves 6.

TIRAMISU
Italian chocolate and brandy trifle

3 large fresh eggs, separated
1½ oz caster sugar (40 g)
½ teaspoon ground cinnamon
11 oz mascarpone cheese (300 g)
18–20 sponge finger (boudoir) biscuits
4 oz dark chocolate, finely grated (110 g)
5 tablespoons brandy
¼ pint strong black coffee (150 ml)

Whisk the egg yolks with the sugar and cinnamon until creamy. Now beat in the cheese (use full fat cream cheese if you can't obtain mascarpone, although it's not quite as good.) In another bowl, whisk the egg whites until stiff and shiny, then fold them into the cheese mixture. Mix the brandy and coffee together, then dip half the sponge finger biscuits briefly, one by one, into the liquid, then lay them across the base of a large glass trifle bowl. Do not let the biscuits become too soggy. Spoon half the cheese and egg mixture on top, then cover with 2 oz (55 g) of the grated chocolate. Repeat the layers of brandied biscuits and cheese, and chill in the fridge for several hours, or overnight. When ready to serve, sprinkle the rest of the grated chocolate over the top.
Serves 6–8.

TROPICAL FRUIT PAVLOVA

for the meringue:
5 egg whites
10 oz caster sugar (250 g)
½ teaspoon vanilla essence

for the filling:
½ pint whipping cream (300 ml)
3 bananas
1 fresh mango, peeled and sliced
8 oz seedless grapes, halved (225 g)
2 teaspoons lemon juice
2 oz caster sugar (55 g)

Whisk the egg whites until stiff then gradually add the sugar until smooth and glossy. Beat in the vanilla essence. Draw a 9 inch (23 cm) circle on a square of non-stick baking parchment placed on a baking sheet. Spoon on the meringue, levelling the top and building up the sides slightly. Cook for about two hours at Gas ½, 250 deg F, 130 deg C. Leave to get quite cold and dry in the oven (preferably overnight) then peel off the paper. When ready to serve, whip the cream until stiff, spread a little on the base and spread the remainder around the edge. Peel and slice the bananas and sprinkle with lemon juice, then mix with the grapes and mango. Arrange the fruit in the centre of the pavlova and sprinkle with caster sugar. Serve at once.
Serves 8.

VANILLA ICE CREAM

1 pint silver top milk (600 ml)
1 vanilla pod
6 egg yolks
6 oz sugar (175 g)
1 pint whipping cream (600 ml)

Place the vanilla pod and milk in a saucepan and heat to just below boiling point. Remove from the heat and leave to infuse for half an hour. Now beat the egg yolks and sugar together in a bowl, stir in the milk, and strain back into the pan. Cook gently over a low heat, stirring until it coats the back of a wooden spoon. Do not boil. Pour into a chilled freezer container and freeze for two hours. Remove from the freezer and beat well to break up the ice crystals. Whip the cream lightly and fold in. Return to the freezer, freeze for another two hours, then beat well again. Freeze until firm. When serving, let the ice cream soften in the fridge for about 30 minutes, otherwise it will be too hard to scoop.
Serves 10.

WALNUT TART

I like to make this tart around Christmastime when walnuts are abundant. It freezes well and is delicious hot or cold.

for the pastry:
6 oz plain flour, sifted (175 g)
4 oz butter (110 g)
1 large egg yolk
grated zest of 1 orange
2 oz caster sugar (55 g)

for the filling:
2 oz butter (55 g)
4 oz caster sugar (110 g)
3 large eggs
1 tablespoon golden syrup
2 tablespoons treacle
juice of $\frac{1}{2}$ a large lemon
1 large egg white
4 oz broken walnuts (110 g)
12 walnut halves

To make the pastry, rub in the flour and butter, stir in the egg yolk, sugar and orange zest, and add enough cold water to make a firm dough. Leave to rest, then roll out and use to line a 10 inch (25 cm) tin. Now beat together the butter and sugar, then add the eggs, golden syrup, treacle and lemon juice, and beat in well. Add the broken walnuts. In another bowl, whisk the egg white until it forms stiff peaks, then, using a metal spoon, fold it gently into the walnut mixture. Spoon into the tart shell. Arrange the walnut halves on top. Bake in the oven at Gas 8, 450 deg F, 230 deg C, for 10 minutes, then reduce the heat to Gas 4, 350 deg F, 180 deg C, and continue cooking for a further 25–30 minutes, until the filling is set. Remove the tart from the oven and leave to cool a little before serving. Serve with pouring cream.
Serves 8.

CAKES & BISCUITS

Flour · Sugar · Butter · Raisins · Eggs · Walnuts

CAKES AND BISCUITS

I get more letters and queries on the subject of cakes than I do on any other cooking topic. I guess that you have to be more careful with ingredients and quantities and oven temperatures with cake making than you do with anything else.

I always think that the best recipes are ones that have been passed on by friends or handed down through families; they are "tried and trusted" to borrow a well worn phrase. Many of the recipes in this section come from other people, and have been very popular in the Bristol Evening Post.

The recipes here are all ones I frequently use at home, and they are pretty foolproof. They have to be; life is so hectic that the "bung it all in and stir it around" method is still my favourite one.

The Christmas cake never fails; it has evolved from my mother's own recipe, tried and tested over many years. The spiritus cake also comes from an old newspaper cutting of hers, and I can remember family Christmases taking on a very boozy aspect as we got older and a rum or brandy soaked sponge took its place on the tea table. Now, as my own children grow up, the spiritus cake is becoming part of our own Christmas.

The sticky malt gingerbread comes from my mother-in-law, and is absolutely delicious. It is very sticky indeed, and it's the best gingerbread recipe I've found.

The boiled fruit cake recipe came from an Evening Post reader, who says her family, of Yorkshire extraction, eats it with cheese. I make it regularly, and give it a good strong almond flavour.

All-in-one fruit cake
Almond cake
Birthday cake
Boiled fruit cake
Chocolate cake
Chocolate chip cookies
Christmas cake
Coconut and rum cheesecake
Coconut slices
Date, apple and walnut loaf
Devil's food cake
Dundee cake
Easter biscuits
Eccles cake

Fairy cakes
Ginger biscuits
Lemon sponge
Madeira cake
Orange shortbread
Picnic cake
Raisin tea bread
Scones
Spiritus cake
Sticky malt gingerbread
Swiss chocolate cake
Summer layer gateau
Wholemeal coconut cake

ALL-IN-ONE FRUIT CAKE

4 oz self raising flour (110 g)
4 oz wholemeal self raising flour (110 g)
2 teaspoons baking powder
2 teaspoons ground mixed spice
4 oz soft margarine at room temperature (110 g)
4 oz soft brown sugar (110 g)
8 oz mixed dried fruit (225 g)
2 eggs, beaten
2 tablespoons milk

Grease and base line a 7 inch (18 cm) round cake tin or a 2 lb (1 kg) loaf tin. Sift the flours, baking powder and spices into a large bowl, add the remaining ingredients and beat until thoroughly combined. The mixture should be fairly stiff but, if it looks too heavy, beat in another tablespoon of milk. Turn the mixture into the tin and bake for about 1 hour 40 minutes at Gas 3, 325 deg F, 170 deg C, or until a skewer inserted in the centre comes out clean. Leave to cool in the tin for 10 minutes or so, then turn out and leave to get quite cold on a wire rack.

ALMOND CAKE

This rich cake is delicious as a tea time treat, or served with a compôte of fruit for a posh pudding.

4 oz butter (110 g)
4 oz caster sugar (110 g)
3 eggs
3 oz ground almonds, sifted (75 g)
1½ oz plain flour, sifted (40 g)

Cream the butter and sugar until light and fluffy. Add the ground almonds and beat well. Beat in the eggs one at a time. Fold in the flour. Spoon the mixture into a greased and lined 8 inch (20 cm) cake tin and bake at Gas 4, 350 deg F, 180 deg C, for 45 minutes. When the cake is firm and golden brown, remove from the oven— it won't have risen much— and let it rest in the tin for 10 minutes. Then turn the cake out and allow to finish cooling on a wire rack. Dust with icing sugar before serving.

BIRTHDAY CAKE

8 oz butter, at room temperature (225 g)
8 oz soft brown sugar (225 g)
grated zest of an orange
5 oz plain flour, sifted (150 g)
5 oz self raising flour, sifted (150 g)
5 eggs
1 lb mixed dried fruit, washed and dried (450 g)
2 oz candied peel (55 g)
4 oz glacé cherries, chopped (110 g)
1 tablespoon black treacle

Cream the butter, sugar and orange rind until light and fluffy. Beat in the eggs one by one, adding a little flour with the last two eggs, to prevent curdling. Fold in the rest of the flour, then add the fruit, peel and cherries. Lastly, stir in the treacle. Transfer to a greased and bottom lined 8 inch (20 cm) square or 9 inch (23 cm) round cake tin and bake for about $3\frac{1}{2}$ hours at Gas 2, 300 deg F, 150 deg C, or until a skewer inserted in the middle comes out clean. Leave to cool in the tin, then, when absolutely cold, wrap in greaseproof paper and store for a couple of weeks or more in an airtight tin.

BOILED FRUIT CAKE

8 oz mixed dried fruit (225 g)
4 oz margarine (110 g)
2 eggs, beaten
6 oz demerara sugar (175 g)
2 drops vanilla essence
2 drops almond essence
6 oz wholemeal self raising flour (175 g)

Place the fruit in a saucepan, cover with boiling water, and boil for five minutes. Strain well, then add the margarine to the fruit and chop in with a knife. Add the beaten eggs, sugar and essences. Sift in the flour and mix it all well together. Turn the mixture into a greased 2 lb (1 kg) loaf tin and bake at Gas 3, 325 deg F, 170 deg C, for about $1\frac{1}{4}$ hours; a skewer inserted in the centre of the cake will come out clean when the cake is cooked. Leave to cool in the tin for a few minutes, then turn out and leave to get quite cold on a wire rack. (Note: if you prefer to use wholemeal flour, it works very well in this recipe.)

CHOCOLATE CAKE

6 oz plain chocolate (175 g)
¾ pint milk (450 ml)
6 oz margarine or butter (175 g)
6 oz soft brown sugar (175 g)
3 eggs, separated
12 oz self raising flour, sifted (350 g)
1 teaspoon baking powder

for the filling:
3 oz unsalted butter (75 g)
4 tablespoons milk
12 oz icing sugar, sifted (350 g)
3 tablespoons cocoa powder, sifted

Break the chocolate into pieces and place in a small pan with a little of the milk. Melt the chocolate over a gentle heat, stirring well, then take off the heat and add the rest of the milk. Cream the butter or margarine and sugar together until light and fluffy, then beat in the egg yolks one at a time. Add the sifted flour and baking powder and half the chocolate milk. Beat well, then stir in the rest of the milk. In a separate bowl, whisk the egg whites until stiff, add a tablespoon or two to the chocolate mixture, and stir well to slacken it, then fold in the rest of the whisked whites. Pour into a greased and lined 10 inch (25 cm) round cake tin and bake for 1½ hours at Gas 4, 350 deg F, 180 deg C, or until a skewer inserted in the centre comes out clean. Leave to cool in the tin for half an hour, then carefully turn out and cool on a wire rack. While the cake is cooling, make the filling. Melt the butter and milk together, then beat in the icing sugar and cocoa powder and beat well. Allow to cool, beating every so often to prevent a skin forming. To assemble, slice the cake horizontally in three and cover each layer with the filling, using what's left over for the top and sides.

CHOCOLATE CHIP COOKIES

4 oz soft margarine (110 g)
8 oz soft brown sugar (225 g)
1 egg
few drops vanilla essence
4 oz wholemeal self raising flour, sifted (110 g)
1 oz cocoa powder (25 g)
4 oz chocolate chips, or grated chocolate (110 g)

Cream the margarine and sugar, then beat in the egg. Add the rest of the ingredients and mix well. Put about 24 dessertspoonfuls of the mixture on to three or four greased baking sheets. Space the blobs well apart, to allow for spreading. Press each mound down slightly with the back of a spoon and bake at Gas 5, 375 deg F, 190 deg C, for 15–20 minutes, or until nicely spread out and slightly cracked around the edges. Leave on the trays for 5 minutes then transfer to wire racks and allow to cool.

CHRISTMAS CAKE

1 lb 6 oz currants (625 g)
8 oz raisins (225 g)
8 oz sultanas (225 g)
3 oz glacé cherries (75 g)
3 oz stoned dates (75 g)
4 oz candied peel (110 g)
4 oz flaked almonds (110 g)
14 oz plain flour (400 g)
1 teaspoon each mixed spice and cinnamon
$\frac{1}{2}$ teaspoon freshly grated nutmeg
pinch of salt
12 oz butter (350 g)
12 oz soft brown sugar (350 g)
grated zest of $\frac{1}{2}$ a lemon
6 eggs, beaten
1 tablespoon treacle
2 tablespoons brandy

These quantities are for a 9 inch (23 cm) round or an 8 inch (20 cm) square cake tin. Grease and line the tin with a double thickness of greaseproof paper. Tie a double band of brown paper, coming well above the tin, around the outside.

Wash and dry the fruit, chopping cherries, dates and other large pieces. Mix well in a large bowl. Add the flaked almonds. Sift the flour and spices into another large bowl and add a pinch of salt. Put butter, sugar and lemon zest into a third bowl and cream until pale and fluffy. Add the beaten eggs little by little, beating well with each addition. Add a spoonful of flour with the last egg to prevent curdling.

Gradually fold the flour and spices into the eggs, then fold in the brandy and treacle. Finally, stir in the fruit and nuts. Turn the mixture into the prepared tin, spreading evenly and making sure that there are no air pockets. Make a hollow in the centre so the cake has a reasonably flat surface when cooked. Bake at Gas 2, 300 deg F, 150 deg C, for about 4 hours, or until a thin warmed skewer comes out clean when inserted in the centre. Cover the cake with greaseproof paper after $1\frac{1}{2}$ hours to prevent over-browning. Leave the cake to cool in the tin before turning out.

Prick all over with a skewer and drizzle 2 tablespoons of brandy over it before wrapping in a double thickness of greaseproof paper and then in foil to store. Keep in an airtight container in a cool place, feeding with brandy from time to time. Cover with marzipan two weeks before Christmas, and ice it a week before.

COCONUT AND RUM CHEESECAKE

2 oz seedless raisins (55 g)
2 tablespoons rum
1 tablespoon lime juice
6 oz coconut biscuits (175 g)
2 oz desiccated coconut (55 g)
3 oz butter (75 g)
10 oz cream cheese (275 g)
$\frac{1}{4}$ pint double cream (150 ml)
4 oz caster sugar (110 g)

Start by putting the raisins to soak in the rum and lime juice. Now make the cheesecake base: melt the butter, crush the biscuits well, and combine melted butter, crushed biscuits, and desiccated coconut. Press into the base of a greased loose bottomed 10 inch (25 cm) flan tin and leave in the fridge for 1 hour or until firm. Now beat the cream cheese, cream and sugar together, then beat in the rum and lime juice, and lastly stir in the plumped up raisins. Spoon this mixture on to the coconut biscuit base and chill again until set. For a special occasion, you could decorate the top with toasted coconut or thin slices of lime.
Serves 8.

COCONUT SLICES

3 oz self raising flour, sifted (75 g)
1 oz plus 2 tablespoons desiccated coconut (25 g)
1 teaspoon baking powder
4 oz soft margarine, at room temperature (110 g)
4 oz caster sugar (110 g)
2 large eggs
a few drops vanilla essence
2 tablespoons raspberry jam

Beat together the sifted flour, 1 oz (25 g) coconut, baking powder, soft margarine, caster sugar, eggs and vanilla essence. The mixture should be of a soft, dropping consistency. If it is not, add a little hot water and beat again. Spoon the mixture into a greased Swiss roll tin, and bake for 25 minutes at Gas 4, 350 deg F, 180 deg C, until risen and golden at the edges. Remove from the oven. Melt the jam and brush it over the top of the sponge while still warm, then sprinkle with the two tablespoons of coconut. Cut into squares or slices when cold.
Makes 16–24 pieces.

DATE, APPLE AND WALNUT LOAF

4 oz self raising flour (110 g)
4 oz wholemeal self raising flour (110 g)
1 teaspoon baking powder
4 oz soft margarine, at room temperature (110 g)
4 oz soft brown sugar (110 g)
2 eggs
4 oz dates, pitted and chopped (110 g)
2 oz walnuts (55 g)
1 cooking apple, peeled, cored and roughly grated
3 fl oz milk (75 ml)
½ teaspoon freshly grated nutmeg

Sift the flours and baking powder into a large mixing bowl. Add the margarine, sugar, eggs, milk and nutmeg. Beat well—an electric beater is best at this—then stir in the apple and dates. Save half a dozen walnuts, chop the rest, and stir them in. Spoon the mixture into a greased 2 lb (1 kg) loaf tin, smooth the top, and decorate with the walnut halves in a line down the middle. Bake at Gas 4, 350 deg F, 180 deg C, for 1 hour, or until a skewer inserted in the centre comes out clean. Leave in the tin for 15 minutes, then turn out on to a wire rack to cool.

DEVIL'S FOOD CAKE

3 oz plain flour, sifted (85 g)
3 oz wholemeal flour, sifted (85 g)
½ teaspoon baking powder
1 teaspoon bicarbonate of soda
2 oz cocoa powder (55 g)
4 oz butter or soft margarine at room temperature (110 g)
8 oz caster sugar (225 g)

2 large eggs, beaten
7 fl oz hot water (200 ml)
1 tablespoon golden syrup

for the frosting:
8 oz sugar (225 g)
¼ pint water (150 ml)
pinch of cream of tartar
1 egg white

Sift the flours, baking powder, bicarbonate of soda and cocoa into a large bowl. In another bowl, beat the fat and sugar together until light and fluffy, then gradually beat in the eggs. Add the flour little by little and stir in the water and golden syrup. Divide the mixture between two 8 inch (20 cm) sandwich tins and bake for about 40–45 minutes at Gas 4, 350 deg F, 180 deg C, until well-risen. Leave in the tins for 5 minutes then turn out and cool on a wire rack. Make the American frosting by dissolving the sugar in the water and then boiling to 238 deg F (the soft ball stage; when a drop placed in cold water forms a soft ball.) Now beat in a pinch of cream of tartar, whisk the egg white until stiff and whisk that in too. Use at once to sandwich the cakes together and to ice the sides and top, using a knife to bring the icing up to pretty peaks and swirls.

DUNDEE CAKE

4 oz each sultanas, currants, and raisins (110 g each)
2 oz blanched almonds, chopped (55 g)
2 oz candied peel (55 g)
8 oz butter or hard margarine at room temperature (225 g)
8 oz light soft brown sugar (225 g)
grated zest of one lemon
4 eggs, beaten
10 oz plain flour, sifted (175 g)

to decorate:
1 oz blanched almonds, split (15 g)

Place the currants, sultanas, raisins, chopped blanched almonds, and candied peel in a large bowl and sprinkle over a couple of tablespoonfuls of the flour. Mix well. In another bowl, cream the butter or margarine with the sugar until pale and fluffy. Beat in the lemon zest. Add the eggs, little by little, beating well after each addition. Gently fold in the sieved flour, then add the fruit and nut mixture. Turn into a greased and bottom lined 8 inch (20 cm) round cake tin, smooth the top, and arrange the split blanched almonds on top. Bake at Gas 3, 160 deg F, 325 deg C, for $2-2\frac{1}{2}$ hours. Cover with foil or several layers of greaseproof paper after the first hour if the top looks like browning too much. Test by inserting a skewer into the cake—if it comes out clean, the cake is ready. Cool in the tin for 15 minutes, then turn out and finish cooling on a wire rack.

EASTER BISCUITS

4 oz unsalted butter or margarine (110 g)
4 oz caster sugar (110 g)
1 egg, beaten
8 oz plain flour, sifted (225 g)
2 oz currants (55 g)
grated zest of $\frac{1}{2}$ a lemon or $\frac{1}{2}$ a teaspoon mixed spice or $\frac{1}{2}$ a teaspoon ground cinnamon
1-2 tablespoons milk or brandy
a little extra caster sugar for dusting

Cream the fat and the sugar until light and fluffy. Beat in the egg, then fold in the sifted flour along with the currants and lemon zest or spice. Mix until the dough is nice and soft, adding a little milk or brandy as necessary. Roll out thinly on a floured surface, and cut out rounds with a biscuit cutter—the bigger the better, I think. Then place the rounds on greased baking trays and bake at Gas 6, 400 deg F, 200 deg C, for about 20 minutes or until golden. Cool on a wire rack and then dust with caster sugar. Store in an airtight tin.
Makes 16-24.

ECCLES CAKES

12 oz ready made puff pastry, thawed if frozen (350 g)
2 oz butter (55 g)
4 oz soft brown sugar (110 g)
4 oz currants (110 g)
½ teaspoon mixed spice
¼ teaspoon freshly grated nutmeg
milk and caster sugar

Roll out the pastry so that you can cut out a dozen 4 inch (10 cm) rounds. Cream the butter and sugar, then mix in the currants, spice and nutmeg. Place about 2 teaspoonfuls of this mixture on each pastry circle. Brush the edges of each circle with water, then fold over and press the sides together with your fingertips, so you have a half-moon shape. (Alternatively, bring four sides up to the centre and press together, then turn over and press down so you have a round shape.) Make two slits in the top of each cake with a sharp knife. Brush each cake with milk, dust with caster sugar, then place on a dampened baking sheet. Bake for 12–15 minutes at Gas 7, 425 deg F, 220 deg C, until golden brown. Cool on a wire rack. Makes 12.

FAIRY CAKES

4 oz unsalted butter or hard margarine, at room temperature (110 g)
4 oz caster sugar (110 g)
2 eggs, beaten
4 oz self raising flour, sifted (110 g)

Options:
2 oz chocolate chips (55 g)
2 oz glacé cherries (55 g)
2 oz chopped dates (55 g)
2 oz sultanas (55 g)
2 oz crystallized ginger (55 g)

to ice:
4 oz icing sugar, sifted (110 g), and colouring and/or flavouring

Arrange 18 to 24 paper cake cases on a baking sheet and preheat the oven to Gas 5, 375 deg F, 190 deg C. Cream the butter or margarine with the sugar until light and fluffy, then add the eggs little by little, beating well after each addition, and add a tablespoon of flour with the last of the egg. Fold in the rest of the sifted flour with a metal spoon. Do not beat. If you are adding chocolate chips or one of the other variations, fold them in now. The mixture should be slack and soft; if it is stiff, mix in a tablespoon of warm water. Spoon into the paper cases so they are about two-thirds full, and then bake for 15–20 minutes until golden. Cool on a wire rack. To ice, beat the icing sugar with a tablespoon of hot water added little by little, and beat in flavouring and/or colouring. Ice when the cakes are cold.

GINGER BISCUITS

4 oz self raising flour (110 g)
1 heaped teaspoon ground ginger
1 teaspoon bicarbonate of soda
1½ oz sugar (40 g)
2 oz margarine (55 g)
2 tablespoons golden syrup

Sift the flour, ginger and bicarbonate of soda into a mixing bowl, then stir in the sugar and rub in the margarine until the mixture resembles breadcrumbs. Add the syrup and mix the ingredients together to form a stiff paste—this is easiest to do with your fingertips. When the mixture is smooth, divide it into about 16 pieces, and form each into a ball. Place on greased baking sheets, fairly widely spaced as they will spread while cooking, and flatten each ball slightly with the back of a spoon. Bake at Gas 5, 375 deg F, 190 deg C, for 10–15 minutes, until lightly browned. Cool on a wire rack before eating or storing. (For a change, and a milder taste, try substituting mixed spice for the ginger.)

LEMON SPONGE WITH FRESH LEMON CURD

4 oz self raising flour, sifted (110 g)
4 oz caster sugar (110 g)
4 oz soft margarine, at room temperature (110 g)
1 teaspoon baking powder
2 large eggs
grated zest and juice of ½ a lemon

for the lemon curd:
2 eggs
grated zest and juice of a large lemon
3 oz caster sugar (75 g)
2 oz unsalted butter (55 g)

To make the cake, put all the cake ingredients into a large mixing bowl and beat well, preferably with an electric beater, for 2 minutes until everything is well combined. The mixture should be of a soft dropping consistency; if it is stiff, add a little extra lemon juice or water and beat again. Divide the mixture between two greased and lined 7 inch (18 cm) sponge tins and cook for 30 minutes at Gas 3, 325 deg F, 170 deg C. Leave to cool in the tins for a few minutes before turning out on to a wire rack. While the cakes are cooking, you can be making the lemon curd. Whisk the eggs in a medium sized bowl, then add the lemon zest and juice, sugar and butter. Place the bowl over a pan containing gently simmering water, and stir until the butter melts. Leave until the mixture thickens, stirring now and then. This will take about 15 minutes. Allow to cool, then use to sandwich the cooled cakes together.

MADEIRA CAKE

6 oz unsalted butter, at room temperature (175 g)
6 oz caster sugar (175 g)
grated zest of two lemons
3 eggs
4 oz plain flour, sifted (110 g)
4 oz self raising flour, sifted (110 g)
1 tablespoon lemon juice

Beat the butter with the sugar until light and fluffy. Stir in the grated lemon rind. Whisk the eggs then beat them into the butter mixture little by little, and, when well blended, fold in the sifted flours. Add the lemon juice if you need to in order to obtain a soft dropping consistency; if the mixture is already nice and soft, leave it out. Turn the mixture into a greased and bottom lined 7 inch (18 cm) round cake tin and bake for 1 hour at Gas 4, 350 deg F, 180 deg C. Leave to cool in the tin for 15 minutes, then turn out and finish cooling on a wire rack. For a really authentic touch, pop a couple of strips of citron peel on top of the cake after it has begun to set, about half way through the cooking time.

ORANGE SHORTBREAD

4 oz unsalted butter (110 g)
2 oz caster sugar (55 g)
finely grated zest of an orange
2 oz cornflour (55 g)
4 oz plain flour, sifted (110 g)

Cream the butter and sugar together until light and fluffy, then beat in the grated orange zest. Sift the flour and cornflour together, then mix into the creamed mixture. Knead a little until smooth, then roll out to a circle about 7 or 8 inches (18–20 cm) in diameter. Place on a greased baking sheet, pinch up the edges to decorate, and prick with a fork. You could also use a greased flan or pie dish, and press the shortbread down into that, which will give you a more accurate circle. Bake for about 35 minutes at Gas 4, 350 deg F, 180 deg C. Cut into eight wedges while still warm, then leave to get cold on the tray or in the tin. (For a change, you could try flavouring the shortbread with lemon zest, or a teaspoon of rosewater.)

PICNIC CAKE

8 oz butter or margarine (225 g)
8 oz caster sugar (225 g)
4 eggs
8 oz plain flour, sifted (225 g)
4 oz self raising flour, sifted (110 g)
1 lb sultanas (450 g)
2 oz almonds, blanched and chopped (55 g)
2 oz glacé cherries, washed and chopped (55 g)
½ teaspoon vanilla essence
¼ teaspoon almond essence
juice and grated zest of a lemon

Cream the butter and sugar until soft. Add the eggs one at a time, beating well with each addition. Sift the flours and fold into the mixture alternately with the fruit, almonds, essences, lemon zest and juice. Mix well, adding a little warm water if necessary; the mixture should remain fairly stiff. Turn into a greased and lined 8 inch (20 cm) cake tin and bake for 1 hour at Gas 4, 350 deg F, 180 deg C, then reduce the heat to Gas 3, 325 deg F, 170 deg C, for another half an hour. Leave to cool in the tin, then turn out. This cake keeps well in an airtight tin.

RAISIN TEA BREAD

This is an old recipe, as you can tell from the teacup measuring system. It doesn't matter what size cup you use as long as you use the same one all the way through.

4 teacups self raising flour
3 teaspoons baking powder
½ teaspoon ground cinnamon
1 teacup raisins
½ teacup brown sugar
2 teacups milk
2 eggs, beaten

Sift the flour, baking powder and cinnamon into a mixing bowl. Add the sugar and fruit and mix well. Pour in the eggs and milk and beat well until smooth. Divide the mixture between two well greased 2 lb (1 kg) loaf tins so that they are not more than three quarters full. Bake at Gas 7, 425 deg F, 220 deg C for 20 minutes, then reduce the heat to Gas 4, 350 deg F, 180 deg C, for another 10 minutes, or until the top is nicely browned. Leave to cool in the tins for a few minutes, then turn out on to a wire rack to get cold. Serve sliced and spread with unsalted butter.

SCONES

8 oz self raising flour, sifted (225 g)
2 oz unsalted butter (55 g)
1 oz caster sugar (25 g)
¼ pint milk (150 ml)

Rub in the flour and butter. Stir in the sugar. Stir in the milk with a round-bladed knife until the mixture binds together. Knead lightly and quickly on a floured surface, then roll out until about 1 inch (2.5 cm) thick. Cut out 6 or 7 scones with a 2½ inch (6 cm) cutter, then roll again and cut out 3 or 4 more. Do not be tempted to roll the dough too thinly; scones do not rise much and if you cut out too many they will look thin and mean. Place on a greased baking tray, brush with milk, and cook for 10-15 minutes at Gas 7, 425 deg F, 220 deg C.

SPIRITUS CAKE

5 oz plain flour, sifted (125 g)
1 oz cocoa powder (25 g)
2 level teaspoons baking powder
5 oz soft dark brown sugar (125 g)
2 large eggs
6 tablespoons corn oil
6 tablespoons milk
½ teaspoon vanilla essence

for the syrup:
4 oz granulated sugar (110 g)
¼ pint water (150 ml)
2 tablespoons rum

for the decoration:
½ pint double cream (300 ml)
4 oz plain chocolate, grated (110 g)

Sift the flour, cocoa powder and baking powder into a large bowl. Add the sugar and mix well. Separate the eggs. Add the corn oil, milk and vanilla essence to the yolks. Make a well in the centre of the dry ingredients and pour in the liquid. Beat well to make a smooth batter. Whisk the egg whites until stiff, then fold into the batter. Pour into a greased and lined 2 lb (1 kg) loaf tin, and bake at Gas 4, 350 deg F, 180 deg C for 40-45 minutes until the cake is beginning to shrink away from the sides. Allow to cool in the tin for a few minutes, then turn out and allow to get quite cold on a wire rack. Now make the syrup. Boil the sugar and water together for five minutes, then take off the heat and stir in the rum. Put the cake back into the tin in which it was baked (line the tin first with a long overhanging strip of foil to help take it out afterwards), and prick it all over with a fork. Pour the hot syrup over and leave overnight to soak up the juices. Decorate with whipped cream and grated chocolate just before serving.
Serves 6-8.

STICKY MALT GINGERBREAD

3 oz plain flour, sifted (75 g)
3 oz wholemeal flour, sifted (75 g)
2 teaspoons baking powder
½ teaspoon bicarbonate of soda
2 teaspoons ground ginger
½ teaspoon mixed spice
2 oz unsalted butter (55 g)
2 oz soft dark brown sugar (55 g)
1 tablespoon black treacle
1 tablespoon golden syrup
1 tablespoon malt extract
7 fl oz milk (200 ml)
2 eggs, beaten
2 oz stem ginger, chopped (55 g)

Sift the flours, spices, baking powder and soda into a bowl. In another bowl, beat together the butter, sugar, treacle, syrup and malt extract. Beat in the milk and eggs, and then stir in the flour and stem ginger. Mix well, then pour the mixture into a greased and lined 8 inch (20 cm) square tin and bake for about 40–45 minutes at Gas 3, 325 deg F, 160 deg C until well risen. Leave to cool for 10 minutes in the tin, then turn out and finish cooling on a wire rack. This gingerbread is delicious as it is, but may also be served with a little lemon icing. To make this, mix the juice of a small lemon with 2 or 3 tablespoons of sifted icing sugar, then pour over the gingerbread and allow to set.

SUMMER LAYER GATEAU

for the sponges:
6 oz self raising flour, sifted (175 g)
6 fresh eggs
6 oz caster sugar (175 g)
few drops vanilla essence
2–3 tablespoons hot water

for the filling:
8 oz raspberries (225 g)
8 oz strawberries (225 g)
½ pint double cream (300 ml)
4 oz mixed chopped nuts (110 g)

Line two Swiss roll tins with baking parchment. Whisk the sugar and eggs in a bowl set over a pan of hot water until thick and creamy. Lightly fold in the flour, then add the water and vanilla essence. Divide the mixture between the two tins and bake at Gas 7, 425 deg F, 220 deg C, for 7–9 minutes. Remove from the oven, allow to cool a little, then turn out on to wire racks. When cold, slice each sponge in half. Beat the cream until thick, then use half of it to sandwich the layers together, adding half the raspberries and strawberries as you go. Spread the rest of the cream on the top and sides, then roll the sides in chopped nuts. Arrange the remaining fruit on top, and serve. (If you cook the sponge early and freeze it, it is actually much easier to assemble the cake while it is still half frozen.)
Serves 6–8.

SWISS CHOCOLATE CAKE

2 oz dark chocolate (55 g)
4 oz unsalted butter (110 g)
4 oz caster sugar (110 g)
4 oz ground almonds (110 g)
2 oz self raising flour, sifted (55 g)
2 large fresh eggs

for the topping:
4 oz dark chocolate (110 g)
2 oz unsalted butter (55 g)
8 walnut halves (optional)

Break up the chocolate for the cake, put it into a mixing bowl and allow to melt over a pan of hot water. Allow the chocolate to cool a little when it has melted, then cream in the butter and sugar. Add the eggs separately, beating well each time. Add the almonds, and beat again. Finally fold in the flour. Spoon the mixture into a greased and lined 9 inch (20 cm) cake tin, and cook at Gas 4, 350 deg F, 180 deg C, for 45–50 minutes. Allow the cake to cool in the tin for a few minutes, then remove and finish cooling on a wire rack. When the cake is cold, make the topping: melt the butter and chocolate together, then allow to cool and thicken. When cold, beat until it shines. Cover the cake with this, making pretty wavy patterns with a fork, and decorate with walnut halves if using.

WHOLEMEAL COCONUT CAKE

6 oz margarine or butter (175 g)
4 oz caster sugar (110 g)
3 eggs
8 oz wholemeal self raising flour, sifted (225 g)
4 oz desiccated coconut (110 g)
¼ pint milk (150 ml)
few drops vanilla essence

Cream the butter or margarine with the caster sugar until light and fluffy. Beat in the eggs one at a time, adding a little of the flour with the last egg. Fold in the rest of the sifted flour, not forgetting all the little grainy bits in the bottom of the sieve, and then fold in the desiccated coconut. Add the vanilla essence and enough milk to form a dropping consistency. Spoon the mixture into a lined and greased 2 lb (1 kg) loaf tin, smooth the top, and bake at Gas 4, 350 deg F, 180 deg C for $1\frac{1}{4}$–$1\frac{1}{2}$ hours; a skewer inserted in the centre should come out clean. If you prefer to make two smaller loaves, divide the mixture between two prepared 1 lb (450 g) loaf tins, and cook for 45–60 minutes. Allow to cool in the tin/s for ten minutes, then turn out and cool on a wire rack.

PRESERVES

Rhubarb · Marrow · Cucumber · Gooseberry · Plums · Onions

PRESERVES

Home preserving is a dying art, I fear, now that most foods, of varying quality, are available all year round, and anything else is canned, frozen or dried.

And although I hate to see garden produce go to waste, I have learned after many trips to the compost heap, flinging out marrow chutney and huge pickled beetroots, that there's no use preserving anything that's not in peak condition to start with; and there's no use making things that people won't eat.

So, I make masses of pickled onions, because we all eat those, but I no longer make runner bean chutney, because no one eats that, except possibly the old folk who end up with it after the local harvest festival. But I do make masses of pickled dill cucumbers, because I live on them, with bread, for lunch in the summer.

I always make marmalade, because mine is better than anything I can buy. And I always make redcurrant jelly not only because it is good for glazing fruit pies but also because it just looks so beautiful shining in its little glass pots in the cupboard, a memory of the summer gone by.

Autumn jelly
Beetroot and onion pickle
Blackcurrant jam
Elderflower and gooseberry jelly
Gooseberry jam
Greengage jam
Green tomato chutney
Mango chutney
Marmalade
Marrow and apple chutney
Mint jelly
Onion chutney

Piccalilli
Pickled dill cucumbers
Pickled onions
Pickled peaches
Plum chutney
Prunes in Armagnac
Raspberry jam
Redcurrant jelly
Rhubarb chutney
Spiced damsons
Tomato chutney
Whizz bang Willenham cider

AUTUMN JELLY

2 lb elderberries (900 g)
2 lb blackberries (900 g)
1 lb cooking apples (450 g)
1 lb plums and/or damsons (450 g)
2 pints water (1 litre)
1 inch (2.5 cm) piece cinnamon stick
½ teaspoon ground ginger
½ teaspoon ground cloves
granulated sugar

Wash all the fruit. Use a fork to strip the elderberries from their stalks. Cut the apples into pieces, discarding any bad bits, but keeping skins, core, pips, etc. Put everything except the sugar into a large preserving pan and cook gently until the apples are soft (about an hour). Strain everything through a jelly bag (or piece of muslin or gauze suspended from an upturned stool) over a large bowl; leave to drip overnight. Do not squeeze the bag. Next day, measure the juice in the bowl, and allow 1 lb (450 g) sugar to every pint (600 ml) juice. Dissolve the sugar gently in the juice, and when it has all dissolved, turn up the heat and boil hard until setting point is reached; start testing after 5 minutes' boiling time. Pour into small sterilized jars, seal, label, and store in a dark place.

BEETROOT AND ONION PICKLE

2 lb beetroot (1 kg)
2 pints malt vinegar (1.2 litres)
½ oz each of black peppercorns, allspice berries and cinnamon stick (15 g each)
¼ oz cloves (8 g)
1 teaspoon salt
4 red onions, peeled and thinly sliced

Place the beetroot, in their skins, in a large pan, cover with boiling water and boil until soft. Meanwhile, simmer the vinegar with the spices for 15 minutes then leave to stand for 2 or 3 hours. Strain, discarding the spices. Slip the skins off the beetroot when they are cooked and cool enough to handle. Slice them neatly, halving if necessary, and pack into preserving jars in alternate layers with the thinly sliced onion. Pour the cold spiced vinegar into the jars, covering beetroot and onion, and seal tightly. Store in a dark place. This pickle may be eaten almost immediately but the flavours will deepen after a few weeks.

BLACKCURRANT JAM

4 lb blackcurrants (2 kg)
3 pints water (1.6 litres)
6 lb sugar (3 kg)

Wash the fruit and remove all the little brown stalks. Some people also remove the little brown remains of the flowers, but this is a fiddly job and I usually don't bother unless they are very large. Life is short, after all. Put the fruit into a pan with the water and simmer very gently until the fruit is soft. Allow plenty of time, and stir occasionally or the fruit will stick and burn. When the currants are soft, stir in the sugar and allow to dissolve. Turn up the heat and boil hard to setting point; blackcurrants contain a lot of pectin and don't usually take long. (If you don't have a sugar thermometer, place a little jam on a plate and allow to cool; push with your little finger, and if it wrinkles, it is set.) Pour the jam into warmed sterilized jars, seal, label, and store in a dark place.

ELDERFLOWER AND GOOSEBERRY JELLY

Fresh elderflowers smell pretty vile, but when cooked they have a delicate grapey aroma. You can use this jelly as an unusual glaze for delicate fruit tarts; or for brushing chicken, lamb or mackerel before grilling or barbecuing.

4 lbs green gooseberries (2 kg)
2 pints water (1.2 litres)
approx 2 lbs sugar (900 g)
5 fresh elderflower heads

Wash the gooseberries and place in a preserving pan with the water. Bring to the boil, then simmer, uncovered, until the fruit is very soft. Put the pulp into a sterilized jelly bag or muslin cloth tied at the corners and suspend overnight over a large bowl to catch the clear juices. Next day, measure the juice back into the pan, and stir in 1 lb sugar (450 g) for every 1 pint (600 ml) of the juice. Shake the elderflowers well, then tie loosely in muslin and put in the pan. Heat slowly until the sugar dissolves, then turn up the heat and boil fast to obtain a set. Gooseberries set quickly, so take care not to overboil. Remove the elderflowers, then pour the jelly into warm sterilized jars, seal, label and store in a cool dark place.

GOOSEBERRY JAM

6 lb gooseberries (3 kg)
6 lb granulated sugar (3 kg)
2 pints water (1.2 litres)

Wash and top and tail the gooseberries, then put them into a large pan with the water. Simmer gently for 30 minutes, or until soft, stirring and mashing them up. Stir in the sugar, and keep stirring over a gentle heat until it has dissolved. Now turn the heat up and boil hard until setting point is reached. This should not take long as gooseberries set well. Test with a sugar thermometer; or by placing a drop on a saucer, cooling, then pushing with your little finger—if it wrinkles, the jam is set. Pour into warmed sterilized jars, seal, label, and store in a cool dark place.

GREENGAGE JAM

6 lb greengages (3 kg)
1 pint water (600 ml)
6 lb sugar (3 kg)

Wash the greengages and cut them in half. Remove the stones and crack a dozen or so. Take out the kernels and blanch in boiling water for a couple of minutes. Slip off their skins and cut the kernels in half. Place the white kernels, halved greengages and the water into a preserving pan and simmer gently until the fruit is soft and pulpy. It helps if during this time you warm the sugar in the oven; your preserving jars can go in too. Tip the sugar into the pan when the fruit is pulpy, heat gently to dissolve the sugar, and then turn up the heat. Boil hard to reach setting point; start testing after 10–15 minutes. Test for setting with a sugar thermometer or by dropping a little jam on to a cold saucer and allowing to cool; push with your finger, and if the jam wrinkles and forms a skin, it is set. Skim if necessary, stir, then pour into warmed sterilized jars. Seal, label and store in a cool dark place.

GREEN TOMATO CHUTNEY

5 lb green tomatoes, sliced (2.3 kg)
1 lb onions, peeled and chopped (450 g)
½ oz freshly ground black pepper (15 g)
1 oz salt (25 g)
1 lb soft brown sugar (450 g)
1 pint malt vinegar (600 ml)
8 oz seedless raisins (225 g)
8 oz sultanas (225 g)
½ oz ground ginger (15 g)

Put the sliced tomatoes and chopped onions into a bowl with the pepper and salt. Mix well, then leave to stand overnight. Next day, put the sugar and vinegar into a pan, heat gently until the sugar dissolves, and then add the raisins, sultanas and ground ginger. Bring to the boil, then turn down the heat a little and allow to bubble quickly for five minutes. Now add the tomatoes and onions and simmer for an hour or so until golden brown and thick. Stir occasionally to prevent sticking. The chutney is ready when the mixture starts to spit rather than bubble. Pour into hot jars, cover, label, and seal.

MANGO CHUTNEY

5 lb mangoes, peeled, stoned and chopped (2.3 kg)
1 lb onions, peeled and chopped (450 g)
1 lb cooking apples, peeled, cored and chopped (450 g)
2 cloves garlic, crushed
2 tablespoons mustard seeds
1 oz salt (15 g)
½ oz ground ginger (8 g)
2 pints white wine vinegar (1.2 litres)
1 lb golden granulated sugar (450 g)

Put the chopped mango, onions, garlic and apple into a preserving pan with 1½ pints (850 ml) water. Bring slowly to the boil, then reduce the heat and simmer for 10–15 minutes or until the mangoes and apples are pulpy and the onion soft. Stir in the mustard seeds, salt, ginger, and half the vinegar and simmer for about an hour, stirring to prevent sticking and burning. Add the sugar and the rest of the vinegar and allow the sugar to dissolve. Bring to the boil, then reduce to a simmer again and bubble gently for 45–60 minutes until nice and thick. Skim if necessary. Pot in warmed sterilized jars, seal, label and store in a cool dark place. Keep for at least six weeks before consuming with curries or cold meats.

MARMALADE

1 lb fresh Seville oranges (450 g)
2 pints water (1.2 litres)
2 lb sugar (900 g)
2 lemons

Wash the oranges and lemons, then simmer very gently in the water in a large covered pan. Allow 2 or 3 hours. When the fruit is very soft and squishy, take it out of the water, cut in half, scrape out the flesh, pith and pips, and return to the pan. Cover the pan again and keep simmering while you chop the peel. Strain the liquid, discarding pith and pips, and return to a preserving pan. Add the sugar to the juice and dissolve it over a gentle heat,. Add the chopped peel, turn up the heat and start boiling. Start to test for a set after 10 minutes. If you don't have a sugar thermometer, place a drop of marmalade on a plate, allow to cool, then push with your little finger; if it wrinkles and forms a skin, it is ready. If not, keep boiling. When set, cool in the pan for 20 minutes, stirring now and then, and then pot in warmed sterilized jars. Seal, label and store in a cool dark place.

MARROW AND APPLE CHUTNEY

2 lb marrow (900 g)
3 oz salt (75 g)
4 lb cooking apples (1.8 kg)
1 lb onions, peeled and chopped (450 g)
8 oz sultanas (225 g)
8 oz raisins (225 g)
1 oz ground ginger (25 g)
$\frac{1}{2}$ oz freshly grated nutmeg (15 g)
$1\frac{1}{2}$ oz English mustard powder (40 g)
$\frac{1}{2}$ oz turmeric (15 g)
6 chillis
$2\frac{1}{2}$ lb sugar (1.2 kg)
$2\frac{1}{2}$ pints malt vinegar (1.5 litres)

Peel, deseed and chop the marrow, place in a large plastic or glass bowl, sprinkle with the salt and leave overnight. Next day, rinse thoroughly, and pat dry. Peel, core and chop the apples. Now place the marrow and all the other ingredients in a large preserving pan and simmer gently. Stir occasionally. It will take 2 or 3 hours to become thick and golden; when it starts to spit rather than bubble it is ready. Spoon into clean warmed preserving jars and store in a cool dark place. Leave for four weeks before consuming with cold meats, cheese, and curries.

MINT JELLY

2 lb cooking apples (1 kg)
1½ pints water (900 ml)
8 fl oz white wine vinegar (225 ml)
about 1 lb sugar (450 g)
1 large bunch of mint, washed
a few drops green food colouring (optional)

Cut any bruises or bad bits out of the apples, wash them, and chop roughly. Place the apples, pips, peel and all, in a large pan with the water and vinegar. Add the mint. Simmer very gently, stirring now and then, until the apples are pulpy. Strain through a jelly bag or clean tea towel suspended above a bowl. Leave the juice to drip overnight; do not squeeze the bag. Next day, measure the liquid; you should have about 1 pint (600 ml). Allow 1 lb (450 g) sugar to every pint of liquid, and place in a large pan. Dissolve the sugar gently. Turn up the heat when the sugar has dissolved, and boil to setting point; start testing after about 8 minutes. You may need to skim off scum if it rises during the boiling. Stir in the food colouring, if you are using it, and pour the jelly into small, clean, warmed jars. Cover and seal at once, label and store in a dark place. Makes about 1 lb (450 g).

ONION CHUTNEY

4 lb onions, peeled and sliced (2 kg)
1½ lb dark brown sugar (700 g)
14 oz raisins (400 g)
¾ pint dry white wine (450 ml)
2–3 cloves garlic, crushed
8 oz stem ginger, chopped small (225 g)
1 teaspoon ground ginger
½ teaspoon curry powder
4–6 cloves
salt and freshly ground black pepper

Place all the ingredients in a large pan and simmer for about 2 hours, stirring occasionally to make sure that things aren't sticking to the bottom. The chutney is ready when it starts to spit rather than bubble and when it is thick and dark brown. Spoon into warmed sterilized jars. Remove the cloves, if you can find them, and discard. Label and store in a dark place.

PICCALILLI

3–4 courgettes or 1 medium marrow
1 medium cauliflower
1 cucumber
1 lb French beans or runner beans (450 g)
1 lb button onions (450 g)
1 oz salt (25 g)
10 oz sugar (250 g)
2 pints white vinegar (1.2 litres)
1 inch piece root ginger, peeled and crushed (2.5 cm)
2 oz plain flour (55 g)
2 oz English mustard powder (55 g)
$\frac{1}{2}$ oz turmeric (15 g)
$\frac{1}{2}$ oz freshly grated nutmeg (15 g)

Chop the courgettes or marrow into small chunks, removing seeds and pith but leaving the skin on. Break the cauliflower into florets, chop the beans and cucumber, and peel the onions. Mix all the vegetables together in a large bowl, and sprinkle with salt. Leave overnight for the salt to draw off some of the vegetables' excess juices. Next day, rinse the vegetables well and tip out on to a clean tea towel and pat off excess water. Place all the vegetables in a preserving pan. Mix the ginger, flour, mustard powder, turmeric and nutmeg to a paste with a little vinegar. Pour the rest of the vinegar into the preserving pan, and simmer until the vegetables are tender but not mushy. Stir carefully now and then. Add a little hot vinegar to the cold paste, then stir into the vegetables. Simmer for 10 minutes, stirring all the time to prevent burning, then put into preserving jars, seal, label and store in a cool place.

PICKLED DILL CUCUMBERS

2 cucumbers, sliced thinly
1 red onion, peeled and very thinly sliced
2 tablespoons salt
1 teaspoon dried dill, or 2 teaspoons fresh dill, finely chopped
$\frac{3}{4}$ pint white wine vinegar (450 ml)
8 oz caster sugar (225 g)

Put the cucumber and onion in a colander, sprinkle with the salt, and leave for a couple of hours. Rinse, and drain well on kitchen paper, patting with more paper to remove excess moisture. Layer in glass preserving jars, interspersing each layer with a sprinkling of dill. If you have fresh dill growing in the garden, place a flower head on top of each jar. Heat the vinegar and gently dissolve the sugar in it. Bring to the boil, then immediately remove from the heat, and pour over the cucumber and onions. Seal and label. Store in a cool, dark place; best used within 4 months or the cucumber will go soft.

PICKLED ONIONS

2 lb shallots or small onions (1 kg)
1½ oz salt (40 g)
2 pints pickling vinegar (1.2 litres)
6 dried chillis (optional)

Peel the shallots or onions and lay them in a shallow dish. Sprinkle with the salt and leave for 8 hours or overnight. Next day, rinse them thoroughly in a colander under the cold tap, then shake well to remove moisture. Now pack them into pickling jars, inserting the chillis if you like your pickled onions really hot. Cover with the vinegar, seal well, and leave for 4–6 weeks before consuming.

PICKLED PEACHES

These pickled peaches are delicious served with cold meats at Christmas time.

2 lb small peaches (900 g)
½ pint white wine vinegar (300 ml)
1 lb brown sugar (450 g)
1 cinnamon stick
½ oz whole cloves (15 g)
1 oz allspice berries (25 g)

Wash and dry the peaches. Do not use any flawed or bruised fruit. Put the sugar and vinegar in a saucepan and dissolve over a gentle heat. Put the fruit in gently, then tie the spices in a muslin bag and suspend it in the saucepan. Simmer until the peaches are just tender. If the liquid does not entirely cover the fruit in the pan, you should turn the peaches around gently from time to time. Take out the peaches and put into preserving jars. Remove the spices. Boil the liquid for 5–10 minutes until syrupy, and pour over the peaches. Seal at once, and store in a dark cool place.

PLUM CHUTNEY

3 lb plums (1.5 kg)
1 lb carrots (450 g)
6–8 cloves garlic
8 chillis
1 pint vinegar (600 ml)
8 oz raisins (225 g)
8 oz sultanas (225 g)
1 lb soft brown sugar (450 g)
2 teaspoons ground ginger
1 teaspoon ground coriander
$\frac{1}{2}$ teaspoon ground cloves
1 teaspoon salt

Cut up the plums and discard the stones. Mince or finely grate the carrots and crush and chop the garlic and chillis. Place the fruit, carrots and vinegar in a pan and simmer until soft. Stir now and then. Add the rest of the ingredients and simmer for an hour or more until thick and soft. Stir from time to time to make sure the chutney isn't sticking. The chutney is ready when it looks opaque and starts to spit instead of bubble. Spoon into warmed sterilized jars, cover, label and seal. Store in a cool dark place for a couple of months before consuming.

PRUNES IN ARMAGNAC

1 lb prunes (450 g)
6 oz sugar (175 g)
$\frac{1}{4}$ pint Armagnac brandy (150 ml)
1 cinnamon stick

The quantities given are approximate, as the ratio of fruit and liquor depends on how tightly you pack the prunes into the jar, and whether the prunes are stoned or not. I think it is best to use stoned prunes, and the largest, best quality fruit you can find. Wash them and fill your jar or jars three-quarters full. Break the cinnamon stick in two, and insert the pieces among the prunes. Make a sugar syrup by boiling together the sugar and $\frac{1}{4}$ pint (150 ml) water for five minutes. Pour over the prunes. Top up with Armagnac, seal tightly, and leave for at least 2 weeks before consuming. Remove the prunes with a little juice when you need them, and simply top up with more prunes, sugar syrup and Armagnac as required. In this way, the pot will keep going for quite a long time and supply you with an excellent instant pudding for that unexpected guest.

RASPBERRY JAM

6 lb raspberries (2.7 kg)
juice of 1 lemon
6 lb sugar (2.7 kg)

Pick over the raspberries but do not wash them. Place them in a large preserving pan with the lemon juice and simmer very gently for 15–20 minutes. Meanwhile, heat the sugar in a low oven, where you can be warming jam jars at the same time. Tip the sugar into the pan and keep the heat very low until it has completely dissolved. Then turn the heat right up and boil until setting point is reached; start testing after 8 minutes. If you do not have a sugar thermometer, place a drop of jam on a plate, allow to cool, then push gently with your little finger; if the jam wrinkles and forms a skin, it is ready. If not, keep boiling, and test again. When the jam reaches setting point, skim it if necessary, allow to cool for 10 minutes, then pour into the prepared jars. Cover with waxed circles and lids, label, and store in a cool dark place.

REDCURRANT JELLY

3 lb redcurrants (1.3 kg)
1 pint water (600 ml)
sugar

Strip the fruit from its stems using the prongs of a fork. Place the fruit in a pan with the water and simmer very gently until soft. Strain through a jelly bag, muslin, or a clean tea towel suspended over a bowl, and leave overnight. Do not squeeze the bag. Next day, measure the resulting liquid and allow 1 lb (450 g) sugar to each pint (600 ml) juice. Place juice and sugar in a preserving pan and heat very gently until the sugar dissolves. Then boil hard without stirring to reach setting point; this will not take long as redcurrants contain a fair amount of pectin. Test with a sugar thermometer or by placing a drop of jelly on a plate, allowing to cool, and then pushing with your little finger; if the jelly wrinkles and forms a skin, it is ready. Pour into small sterilized jars, seal and label. Store in a cool dark place.

RHUBARB CHUTNEY

3 lb rhubarb (1.3 kg)
2 lb onions, peeled and chopped (900 g)
1 pint white vinegar (600 ml)
1 lb sultanas (450 g)
zest and juice of 2 lemons
1 oz piece root ginger, peeled and crushed (25 g)
2 teaspoons ground mixed spice
1 teaspoon salt
2 lb brown sugar (900 g)

Cut the rhubarb into $\frac{1}{2}$ inch (1 cm) slices, and put into a large preserving pan with the prepared onions. Add half the vinegar, the sultanas, lemon zest and juice, root ginger, salt and mixed spice. Stir well. Simmer for 30–40 minutes until the fruit is very soft. Now add the rest of the vinegar, and the sugar. Stir until the sugar has completely dissolved. Simmer for another $1\frac{1}{2}$ hours, stirring now and then, until the mixture is very thick. Skim if necessary, then spoon into warmed sterilized jars. Seal, label and store in a cool dark place.

SPICED DAMSONS

4 lb large damsons (2 kg)
1 pint malt vinegar (600 ml)
$1\frac{1}{2}$ lb sugar (750 g)
1 inch piece cinnamon stick (2.5 cm)
pinch of mace
6 allspice berries
6 peppercorns

Tie the pickling spices in a small muslin bag or similar. Put the vinegar, sugar and pickling spices into a large pan and simmer gently, stirring occasionally to make sure the sugar dissolves. Wash the fruit, then prick each damson a few times with a darning needle or similar. Add the damsons to the vinegar and cook until soft but not mushy. This will take 10–15 minutes. Take care not to cook for too long as damsons break up very quickly once they become soft. Remove the fruit from the pan with a perforated spoon and pack into hot preserving jars. Boil the vinegar syrup for five minutes until it thickens slightly, remove the spices, and pour over the damsons. Cover tightly and store in a dark place.

TOMATO CHUTNEY

9 lb ripe tomatoes (4 kg)
1 lb onions, peeled and finely chopped (450 g)
6–8 cloves garlic, peeled and crushed
½ pint distilled malt vinegar (300 ml)
1 oz English mustard powder (25 g)
1 teaspoon each salt, mixed spice and paprika
½ teaspoon cayenne pepper
1½ lb sugar (675 g)

Skin the tomatoes by plunging them into boiling water for a few minutes, then remove from the water and slip off the skins. Chop the tomatoes coarsely and place in a large pan with the onions and garlic. Simmer for 15 minutes, stirring, until thick and pulpy. Add vinegar, mustard, salt, spice, paprika and cayenne to the pan and continue simmering, stirring occasionally until thick. Reduce the heat, add the sugar, and allow to dissolve completely. Turn up the heat a little, simmer for another 20 minutes or until thick, stirring often to make sure the chutney doesn't stick to the bottom. Transfer to clean warmed jars, and cover and label. Makes about 6 lb (2.5 kg).

WHIZZ BANG WILLENHAM CIDER

1½ lb apples (700 g)
6 pints cold water (3.6 litres)
1 lb sugar (450 g)
rind and juice of 1 large lemon

Cut any bad bits out of the apples, then grate them coarsely. Place grated apples, peel and cores, in a large clean plastic bucket, add the water, cover with a lid and leave for 1 week. Stir daily. On the seventh day, strain off the juice and discard the apple pulp. Return the juice to the bucket and add the sugar, lemon juice and zest and then leave for 24 hours. Strain, then bottle in beer or cider bottles, and leave for 10 days before drinking.

Note
This semi-sweet drink is extremely fizzy, and although I have used screw topped bottles in the past without incident, it is certainly safer to buy plastic bungs and use those, so if excess gas builds up it can escape rather than exploding the bottle. This wonderful recipe was passed on to me by Mrs Joan Davey, an Evening Post reader, and we now use it every autumn to deal with the usual glut of apples, both cookers and eaters.

INDEX

Aduki bean casserole 108
Afelia (pork with wine and coriander) 96
All-in-one fruit cake 174
Almond cake 174
Anchoïade (Mediterranean anchovy dip) 10
Apple and almond pudding 156
Apple and cheese pork burgers 96
Apricot dacquoise (nutty meringue gateau) 156
Apricot pancakes 157
Artichokes vinaigrette 10
Asparagus with lemon and herb butter 11
Avocado and onion dip 16
Avocados with crab 11
Autumn jelly 192
Autumn lamb stew 91

Baked monkfish 48
Baked red mullet 48
Baked rice pilaff 117
Bean soup 30
Beef and apple casserole 86
Beef and butter bean casserole 86
Beefburgers 87
Beef salad with warm ginger dressing 142
Beetroot and onion pickle 192
Beetroot soup 30
Belgian carbonade (beef braised in ale) 87
Birthday cake 175
Blackcurrant ice cream 157
Blackcurrant jam 193
Blackcurrant strudel 158
Boeuf en daube (bacon-wrapped braised beef) 88
Boiled fruit cake 175
Boston baked beans 108
Brill à la fermière 49
Broad bean soup 31
Broccoli with almonds 124
Brown rice pilaff 117

Cacik 12
Carrot salad 142
Carrot and cauliflower soup 31

Catalan chicken 68
Celery and Stilton soup 32
Cheese puffs 12
Cheesy shrimps 13
Cheesy tricorns 13
Chestnut and chocolate roulade 158
Chicken and avocado salad 143
Chicken and broccoli au gratin 68
Chicken and pineapple salad 143
Chicken cacciatore (Italian style chicken) 69
Chicken chasseur 70
Chicken in cider 71
Chicken liver, mushroom and walnut pâté 14
Chicken liver salad 144
Chicken livers in sour cream 14
Chicken risotto with prawns 71
Chicken with lime and ginger 72
Chicken with prunes and bacon 72
Chicken with tarragon and lemon 73
Chinese chicken and mushroom soup 32
Chinese leaf salad 144
Chinese leaf stir fry 124
Chocolate cake 176
Chocolate chip cookies 176
Chocolate orange mousse 159
Chocolate pears 159
Chocolate strawberry roll 160
Christmas cake 177
Christmas meringue 160
Christmas pudding 161
Coconut and rum cheesecake 178
Coconut slices 178
Cod and broccoli bake 49
Cod Provençale 50
Colcannon 125
Cold poached salmon with watercress sauce 51
Compôte of pears 161
Coriander mushrooms 15
Coronation turkey salad 73
Coq au vin 74
Courgette and nettle soup 33
Courgettes Provençale 125
Creamy potato soup 33
Crispy liver with tartare sauce 102
Cucumber and crab salad 15

Cucumber and mint salad 145
Cucumber soup 34
Curried parsnip soup 34
Curried turkey 74
Custard ice cream 162

Date, apple and walnut loaf 179
Devil's food cake 179
Dips for special occasions 16, 17
  avocado and onion
  garlic and herb
  hummus
  tuna and chick pea pâté
Duck with mango sauce 75
Dundee cake 180

Easter biscuits 180
Eccles cakes 181
Economical pork casserole 97
Elderflower and gooseberry jelly 193

Faggots 102
Fairy cakes 181
Fennel salad 145
Fennel soup 35
Feta and watermelon salad 146
Fish and mushroom pie 52
Fish cakes 52
Fish chowder 53
Fish soup 35
Flaky mushroom and walnut pie 126
French onion soup 36
French peas 126

Garlic and herb dip 16
Garlic beef and vegetable stir fry 88
Gazpacho (iced Spanish tomato soup) 36
German apple slice 162
Ginger biscuits 182
Goat's cheese salad 146
Gooseberry jam 194
Greek leeks 127
Greek lamb goulash (stifado) 95
Green beans in tomato sauce 127
Greengage jam 194
Green risotto 118
Green tomato chutney 195
Grilled summer vegetables 128

Haddock with mushrooms 53
Hake and potato bake 54
Hake in white wine 54

Ham, chicken and mushroom risotto 118
Ham, leek and pea soup 37
Herb and Stilton pâté 18
Honey and ginger spare ribs 97
Hot crab salad 147
Hot new potato salad 128
Hummus 17

Indian beef kebabs 89
Italian liver 103
Italian salmon salad 147
Italian seafood risotto 55
Italian tuna salad 18
Italian winter salad 148

Jerusalem artichoke soup 37

Kedgeree 119
Kidneys turbigo 103
Kohl rabi with cheese 129

Lamb and lentil soup 38
Lamb with rosemary and lemon 91
Lancashire hotpot 92
Leek and potato soup 38
Leafy green salad 148
Lemon sponge with fresh lemon curd 182
Lemon and sardine pâté 19
Lentil and mushroom bake 109
Lentil casserole 109
Lentil soup 39
Lettuce and watercress soup 39
Liver Stroganoff 104

Macaroni carbonara 113
Mackerel in cider 55
Mackerel with herbs 56
Madeira cake 183
Mango chutney 195
Marmalade 196
Marrow and apple chutney 196
Mexican beef tacos 90
Minestrone 40
Mint jelly 197
Mixed bean salad 110
Moules marinière (mussels in white wine) 19
Mushroom and rosemary soup 41
Mussels in tomato sauce 20

Navarin of lamb (Lamb with spring vegetables) 92

Old-fashioned steak and kidney pudding 90
Onion chutney 197
Orange and peanut coleslaw 149
Orange shortbread 183
Oriental fruit salad 163

Pasta and bean soup 41
Pasta Niçoise 113
Pasta with asparagus 114
Pasta with mushrooms 114
Pâté en croûte (pâté in a pastry crust) 20
Pasta with pork and peas 115
Pear and ginger tart 163
Pheasant casserole 75
Piccalilli 198
Pickled dill cucumbers 198
Pickled onions 199
Pickled peaches 199
Picnic cake 184
Plum chutney 200
Pork and cabbage bake 98
Pork escalopes with lemon and tarragon 98
Pork goulash 99
Pork satay with peanut sauce 99
Pork with cider and apples 100
Pork with green olives 100
Pork with wine and coriander (afelia) 96
Potato, celery, and walnut salad 149
Potato gratin dauphinois 129
Poule au pot (chicken casserole) 76
Prawn cocktail with blue cheese dressing 21
Prawn, spinach and mushroom pie 57
Prunes in Armagnac 200

Raan (spicy leg of lamb) 93
Rabbit casserole 77
Rabbit Provençale 77
Raisin tea bread 184
Raspberry and redcurrant tart 164
Raspberry jam 201
Raspberry Malakoff 164
Raspberry roll 165
Red bean chilli soup 42
Redcurrant and almond roulade 165
Redcurrant jelly 201
Rhubarb chutney 202
Rhubarb fool 166

Rice and lentil bake 119
Rice, bean sprout and sweetcorn salad 120
Rice with pistachio nuts 120
Rigatoni with chicken livers 115
Roast leg of lamb with garlic 93
Roast pheasant and game chips 78
Rogan Josh (spicy lamb and tomato casserole) 94
Root vegetables au gratin 130
Rough country paté 21
Runner bean stir fry 130

Salade Niçoise 22
Salmon en croûte (salmon in pastry) 58
Salmon mousse 22
Scones 185
Sea bream meunière 59
Sea bream with apple 59
Seafood salad 150
Seafood thermidor 60
Sesame pork and bean sprout stir fry 101
Skate baked with green olives 61
Skate with black butter 61
Smoked mackerel and dill pâté 23
Smoked salmon nibbles 23
Somerset fish 62
Spanish paella (shellfish, chicken and rice) 62
Special cauliflower cheese 131
Spiced damsons 202
Spiced lamb kebabs 94
Spicy bean and pepper goulash 110
Spicy cauliflower 131
Spicy chicken with yogurt 78
Spicy fish 63
Spicy leg of lamb (raan) 93
Spicy lamb and tomato casserole (rogan Josh) 94
Spicy marrow crumble 132
Spinach and yogurt pie 133
Spinach tart 133
Spiritus cake 185
Spring greens stir fry 134
Spring rolls 24
Steamed ginger pudding 166
Sticky malt gingerbread 186
Stifado (Greek lamb goulash) 95
Stir fried turkey 79
Stir fried lamb with vegetables 95

Stuffed chicken breasts with fresh tomato sauce 79
Stuffed red cabbage 134
Stuffed mushrooms 25
Stuffed plaice fillets 25
Stuffed turkey breasts 80
Summer chicken casserole 80
Summer layer gateau 187
Summer meringue 167
Summer pudding 167
Swiss chocolate cake 187

Tagliatelle turkey 116
Tarragon pork salad 150
Tipsy turkey 81
Tiramisu (Italian chocolate and brandy trifle) 168
Tomato and basil soup 42
Tomato chutney 203
Tomato salad 151
Tomato soufflé 135
Tropical fruit pavlova 169
Trout with herbs and lemon 63

Tuna and chick pea pâté 17
Tuna baked in red wine and herbs 64
Turkey and apple salad 151
Turkey and red bean soup 43
Turkey tikka 81
Turkey with nuts and honey 82

Vanilla ice cream 169
Vegetable soup with dumplings 44
Vegetable crudités 26
Vegetable tagliatelle 116
Vegetarian bake 135
Vegetarian cassoulet 111
Vegetarian chilli 112
Vegetarian cottage pie 112
Vegetable hotpot 137

Waldorf salad 152
Walnut tart 170
Watercress and mushroom roulade 138
Watercress and mushroom salad 152
Whisky prawns 26
Whizz bang Willenham cider 203
Wholemeal coconut cake 188